THE TIMES

TIMES BOOKS

HarperCollins*Publishers*
77–85 Fulham Palace Road
Hammersmith
London W6 9JB

The HarperCollins website address is
www.**fire**and**water**.com

First published 2004

The Times "Questions Answered" column is compiled by Patrick West

Reprint 10 9 8 7 6 5 4 3 2 1 0

ISBN 0 00 719135 9

British Library Cataloguing in Publication Data
A catalogue record for this book is available from the British Library

Text design by Clare Crawford

Printed and bound in Great Britain by Clays Ltd, St Ives plc

CONTENTS

INTRODUCTION

Human beings are a famously inquisitive lot. Indeed, our thirst for knowledge is one of our defining characteristics. We see this instinct in action every day: people reading newspapers in cafés, students making their way to college, astronomers inspecting the heavens, ornithologists scanning the skies, even that pair of insufferable gossips in front of you on the bus just want to know what so-and-so next door is up to. To be human is to ask: "why? what? how?"

It is not merely the profound and pedestrian that consistently confound us ("Why am I here?"; "Why won't my car start?"); we often find ourselves puzzled by that which we had previously taken for granted. As if through a divine spark of curiosity, someone who has attended football games for thirty years will suddenly ponder: "Why do we call a match between two sides a 'local derby'?" A Briton returning from a trip to France might similarly find himself asking: "I wonder why we drive on the left-hand side of the road?" A Saturday afternoon shopper, gazing idly into the window of an antiques store, all of a sudden scratches her head: "Why do clocks with Roman numerals always display the number 4 as IIII rather than IV?"

Since February 2002, readers of *The Times* have been posing such quandaries to its Questions Answered column, challenging fellow readers to furnish them with explanations. This book is a collection of the finest answers – on matters cultural, linguistic, historical, sporting, metaphysical, trivial and satirical. If you have ever wondered who were the original Tom, Dick and Harry, why we clink our glasses before we drink a toast, who was the first military leader to command his men, "Don't shoot until you see the whites of their eyes", or what was really in the briefcase in *Pulp Fiction*, the pages that follow will serve to illuminate.

Knowledge is a virtue. So too is the capacity to refute falsehood. *The Times Book of Questions Answered* investigates and exposes our common assumptions and fallacies. It is said that water goes down the plughole in the opposite direction in the southern hemisphere. Some contend that Henry VIII wrote *Greensleeves*. Folklore also has it that nautical maps in years-gone-by had written at their periphery: "Here Be Dragons". What is the veracity of such urban legends? (The answers to the above are, respectively: no it doesn't; no he didn't; yes, some of them actually did).

This book is for those who seek enlightenment, entertainment and amusement. It is also dedicated to its authors: the public. Enjoy.

Patrick West, Editor, Questions Answered

1. ARMY, NAVY AND MILITARY

Why does the United Kingdom not have a Royal Army when we have a Royal Air Force and a Royal Navy? After all, the Army's crest is dominated by the Crown. And why do some Army regiments have the prefix "Royal" while others do not?

Stanley Blenkinsop, Macclesfield, Cheshire

This is because the Army dates back to feudal times, when the monarch had an army, but so did the other aristocrats. Hence some regiments have the Royal prefix and others do not. Individuals may have owned one or more ships, but the Navy as a unit was only ever owned by the monarch. The RAF was formed by an amalgamation of the Royal Flying Corps (a branch of the Army) and the Royal Naval Air Service in April 1918.

Sebastian Marr, Chippenham, Wiltshire

In my far-off military days an army was a formation composed of several divisions and itself a constituent of an army group. "The Army" was therefore a misnomer, as the Royal Army would have been. To refer in any formal context to "the Army" would have raised the question which Army? In the War Office the usage was H. M. Land Forces.

Douglas Rimmer, Birmingham

When did the last known veteran of Waterloo die? Did any make it to the 20th century?

Dr Jeff Bertucen, Drummoyne, New South Wales

My father, Dr John O'Brien, 1900–81, recounted that he attended the 100th birthday in Millstreet, Co Cork, of John o' the Cross, who had been a young drummerboy at Waterloo and who recalled seeing Wellington and Blucher as he beat the retreat.

J. Fintan O'Brien, Altrincham, Cheshire

In the census return of 1871 for Oxton in the Wirral, against the name Ann Mathews, a 55-year-old widow and seamstress, the enumerator has added a marginal note: "Ann Mathews was born on the march from Quatre Bras to Waterloo." If not the oldest veteran, she was certainly the youngest participant in the campaign.

Mr G. Harrison, Upton, Cheshire

Ann Mathews's birth on the march from Quatre Bras to Waterloo was presumably on the withdawal after the battle, which was fought south of Waterloo, the battle being named after the site of the headquarters — not the field itself. Sadly, therefore, she would not have qualified as a participant in the battle.

Brigadier Bill Bewley, Stranraer, Dumfries and Galloway

The last surviving combatant veteran of Waterloo (on the British side) is believed to have been George Keppel, later 6th Earl of Albemarle, who died in 1891. He took part in the battle, five days after his 16th birthday, as an ensign in the 3rd Battalion, the 14th Foot. Exhausted and ragged, he then marched with the victorious troops to Paris. In his later years he would hold receptions at his daughter's house in Portman Square on each anniversary of Waterloo.

Hinda Rose, London NW1

The French historian Henry Lachouque mentions a Captain Soufflot, who served with the Red Lancers at Waterloo, who died aged 100 in 1893; and Chasseur Vivien, who died at Lyons in 1892, aged 106.

Peter Starr, Radstock, Somerset

In Anne Brown's 1961 adaptation of Commandant Henry Lachouque's famous *Napoléon et la Garde Impériale*, mention is made (page 504) of one veteran living in three centuries. "Lieutenant Markiewcz of the Polish light-horse was born in Cracow in 1794, fought in the Russian campaign, was decorated in 1813, charged at Waterloo, and was still living in 1902". Wow!

Dr James Wright, Yelverton, Devon

Who was the last known survivor of the Battle of Trafalgar?
Dr James Wright, Yelverton, Devon

The last survivor of the Battle of Trafalgar, on the British side, was James Fynmore, who served as a midshipman in the Royal Navy. He later served as a captain in the Royal Marines, and retired as lieutenant-colonel. He died in Peckham, South London, on April 15, 1887, aged 94.

The penultimate British survivor was Admiral Sir George Rose Sartorius, GCB, who also served as a midshipman, in the *Tonnant*, and who died on April 13, 1885, aged 95.

The *Warwick Advertiser* of October 28, 1882 refers to the last survivors of this battle as both of the above officers. James Fynmore is identified as the last survivor by Frederic Boase in *Modern English Biography* (1892). Sartorius is recorded in the *Dictionary of National Biography*.

Richard King, Leamington Spa

John Edwards fought as a boy sailor aged ten at the Battle of Trafalgar in HMS *Victory*. He lived a long life dedicated to communal service: in 1848 he was one of the first Jews elected as a Portsmouth town councillor (Jews were not accorded full civil rights in Britain until 1858), and later he became warden of a synagogue.

John Edwards died on August 18, 1893, aged 98. His great-great-granddaughter married my cousin and the family now live in Israel where Edwards's descendants six generations down the line are serving in the Israeli Army.

Richard Cooper, Gosport, Hampshire

Richard Cooper claims his ancestor, John Edwards, was the last survivor of the Battle of Trafalgar, having served as a ten-year-old on HMS *Victory* and dying in 1893.

I have searched the muster book of HMS *Victory* and can find no John Edwards listed at the Battle of Trafalgar. Nor does his name appear in the Naval General Service medal roll for Trafalgar. The youngest member of HMS *Victory's* crew was Thomas Twichett, aged 12.

John Edwards's obituaries in the *Jewish Chronicle* and the *Hampshire Telegraph* state that he came from London to Portsmouth in 1813. He was a licensed navy agent from 1837 to 1865. There is no mention in his obituary that he served on HMS *Victory* at Trafalgar, or in the Royal Navy.

Graham Hunt, Gosport, Hampshire

I should like to thank Graham Hunt for his contribution to the quest for the last survivor of the Battle of Trafalgar. His points are well made and a classic illustration of the conflict, often faced by researchers, between oral and written records.

My source was John Edwards's own account told to his grandsons Lewis and Naphthali; Lewis's is printed in "Portsmouth Papers No.41: Portsmouth Jewry" published by Portsmouth City Council, while

Naphthali's was told to our family solicitor, a man of impeccable rectitude. Both are identical. However, this is at odds with the records quoted by Mr Hunt. I am further damned by the fact that, while Edwards's age at death makes him born in 1795, his entries in the 1851 and 1881 censuses point to a birth date of 1805.

So I must concede reluctantly that the venerable gentleman made up this exciting tale in old age to entertain his grandchildren, and withdraw him from candidacy for oldest survivor on the British side.

Richard Cooper, Gosport, Hampshire

The last generally agreed survivor was, in fact, Spanish. Pedro Antonio Zía Martínez, a 15-year-old boy seaman aboard the 74-gun, third-rate *San Juan Nepomuceno*, died in Dallas, Texas, on February 1, 1898, at what an obituary called "the respectable age" of 109.

Source: *Trafalgar and the Spanish Navy* by John Harbron (1988).

Mike Windle, Bognor, West Sussex

From where comes the saying "Don't shoot until you see the whites of their eyes"?

June Romaine-Barnard, Dunmow, Essex

This command was given by the American General, William Prescott, as his militia men awaited the attack of the British Army at Bunker Hill, Boston, in June 1775, in one of the earliest battles of the American Revolutionary War. The ragtag American "army" was not a national one, as no nation existed. Instead, the army was made up of men from Massachusetts, Connecticut, New Hampshire and Rhode Island.

In order to beat the British to the high ground outside Boston, Prescott led 1,200 of his often ill-disciplined, disobedient and occasionally intoxicated soldiers to dig in and fortify Bunker Hill under cover of darkness on June 16. When dawn broke, 2,300 troops under the command of Major-General Howe attacked.

As the British troops, in their bright red wool jackets and weighed down by heavy equipment, marched up the hill, the colonists remained calm as Prescott gave that famous order: "Don't shoot until you see the whites of their eyes."

Prescott's order was apparently given both to help to preserve low ammunition supplies and to ensure that the American militia opened fire only within range of their antiquated firearms.

Once the British came within range, the colonists began firing and the British soldiers stated to fall rapidly. The British forces were driven back twice but on their third and final thrust, the British were able to break through the colonists' line, overrunning the tentative American fortifications, and taking the hill. The colonists fled back up the peninsula since it was their only escape route. This battle, which lasted for approximately three hours, was one of the deadliest of the Revolutionary War.

Although the British technically won the battle because they took control of the hill, they suffered too many losses to benefit fully. The British had suffered more than a thousand casualties while the colonists suffered only 400 to 600 casualties from an estimated 2,500 to 4,000 men.

David Malaperiman, Tangley, Hampshire

Further to your previous correspondence, which attributes the saying to the American General William Prescott, at the Battle of Bunker Hill in 1775, this phrase is actually recorded some 32 years earlier.

At Dettingen, Flanders, on June 27, 1743, Lieutenant-Colonel Sir Andrew Agnew of Lochnaw (5th Baronet) gave to the men of his regiment, the 21st of Foot, an order from which this saying is derived. A man of spirit even for the times, he had earlier in the day replied to a brigade order that "the scoundrels will never have the impudence to attack the Scots Fusiliers", but they did.

Formed in square, the Scots Fusiliers held a steady fire rolling along their lines and kept off the advancing French infantry. Sir Andrew, a resourceful and experienced officer, had in training practised a novel battle drill with the men in his square, should they be attacked by cavalry.

At last, the opportunity to spring this trap appeared when the square was attacked by enemy cuirassiers. Instead of employing the orthodox tactic of seeing them off by standing firm and taking the charge on muskets and pikes, Sir Andrew gave orders that as the cavalry approached the front line the two centre companies should divide from the centre and fall back from the outer markers. This novel approach allowed the cavalry to charge through a lane with the Fusiliers facing inwards. At this point Sir Andrew gave the command:

"Dinna fire till ye can see the whites of their e'en . . . if ye dinna kill them they'll kill you." The French, as they rode through this lane of soldiers, were subjected to a withering crossfire and destroyed.

Later in the day King George II, who commanded the Army but was a little out of his depth, rode up and said: "So, Sir Andrew, I hear the cuirassiers rode through your regiment today."

"Ou, ay, yer Majestee," was the reply "but they didna get oot again."

This account is extracted from an article in the *Journal of the Royal Highland Fusiliers* Volume 24, No 2 (Winter 2000) and written by Sir Andrew's descendant, Major Sir Crispin Agnew of Lochnaw, Bt.

Dr J. R. Donald, Glasgow

Where, when and by whom was the term "weapons of mass destruction" first used? At what point does a weapon become massively destructive?

Richard Warner, Warwick

The term "weapons of mass destruction" appears in several postwar arms control treaties, starting with the Outer Space Treaty of January 1967, which referred to "nuclear weapons or any other kinds of weapons of mass destruction". There was no further definition but it was generally understood to include biological and chemical weapons.

Mass destruction can be a misleading phrase. Many chemical and biological weapons would be far less destructive than the incendiaries that razed Dresden. Chemical and biological weapons kill people but do not destroy things. Most conventional ones destroy both. The sarin gas on Tokyo's underground killed relatively very few.

A less extravagant phrase is needed such as NBC (nuclear, biological, chemical) weapons. They will of course remain horrible and indiscriminate and therefore prime targets for arms control.

Stephen Pullinger, London WC2

The term became commonplace in Soviet military science during the 1960s, particularly in relation to the "Revolution in Military Affairs" brought about by the advent of nuclear weapons.

In 1956 the Minister of Defence, Marshal of the Soviet Union, G. K. Zhukov, told the 20th Party Congress of the Communist Party of the Soviet Union: "Future war, if it is unleashed, will be characterised by the mass use of air forces, various rocket weapons and various means of mass destruction such as atomic, thermonuclear, chemical and bacteriological weapons."

Thereafter these various means are referred to in Soviet terminology as weapons of mass destruction.

Sam Pope, Petersfield, Hampshire

Is there any recorded history of anyone "nailing his colours to the mast"?

Colin Bower, Blandford Forum, Dorset

After the top of the mast of Admiral Duncan's flagship was shot away in the Battle of Camperdown in 1797, Jack Crawford climbed up and nailed the colours back to show that they had not surrendered. Crawford was given a special medal for his heroism but when he fell on hard times later it was pawned. He died in the 1832 cholera epidemic in his native town of Sunderland.

George Patterson, Durham

Fifty years ago, when I was living in Sunderland, I used to take a regular walk with two small children to Mowbray Park where there was a very dramatic statue. It was of a barefoot boy in short ragged trousers and an open-necked shirt who was using the butt of his pistol to nail a flag to the mast. The plaque stated "Jack Crawford, the hero of Camperdown, October 11, 1797".

Monica Mann, Bath

This custom stems from the fact that in the past, ships going into battle hoisted their national flag and battle pennant. In the event of a surrender, such flags were hauled down on the captain's orders. However, to guard against the risk of the taut rope being shot away, leaving the flag to tumble to the deck, some unfortunate crew member was sent up aloft to nail the flag in place: hence the expression.

It should be noted that, at times, officers or crewmen would attempt to surrender against the captain's wishes and nails in the flag were something of a deterrent.

Gordon Moore, Littlehampton, West Sussex

A little-known case of this may be found in the battle, on May 27, 1863, between the ironclad river gunboat USS *Cincinnati* and Confederate shore batteries during the siege of Vicksburg, Mississippi, in the American Civil War.

After being holed below the fantail, *Cincinnati* sank in three fathoms of water.

The Congressional Medal of Honour was awarded (in 1916!) to her quartermaster, Frank Bois, who, while under heavy fire, nailed the flag of the United States to her mast, or rather, the stump of one, all three having been shot away — so enabling the vessel to go down with her colours flying.

T. A. Heathcote, Camberley, Surrey

The family of Manwaring Parker have the detailed history of Midshipman Henry Parker of the *Bellisle*, which was very severely damaged at the Battle of Trafalgar.

Midshipman Parker was the ADC to Captain Hargood and he is shown in family pictures hoisting the Union Flag on the demasted ship to signify "no surrender".

He was severely wounded doing this. Captain Hargood and very many other sailors on the ship were also wounded but still the ship fought on in the Nelson tradition.

Parker's prayer book and his application for the Trafalgar medal gives an account of the action.

His direct descendant, Commander John Manwaring Parker, was the lieutenant of the boarding party from HMS *Cossack*, which boarded the *Altmark*. It was he who shouted the "The Navy's here" in order to locate the Merchant Navy prisoners battened below the hatches.

Michael Shortall, Yeovil

What was the purpose of the spikes on the helmets of German soldiers in the 1914–18 war? Were the troops supposed to butt their enemies in the chest? One would suppose that the spikes were most inconvenient, catching in trees, barbed wire and doorways.

Professor Emeritus P. B. Fellgett, Bodmin

The Prussian Army adopted the leather *Pickelhauber* as its standard infantry headdress in 1842. The tall brass spike had ventilation holes near its base, but was otherwise purely ornamental. The shape changed slightly over the years, but in 1914 the German infantryman still took to the field wearing this helmet, albeit shrouded with a drab cloth cover. It was not until the introduction of the steel helmet in 1916 that the *Pickelhauber* ceased to be issued.

It may be of interest that, following the Prussian victory in the Franco-Prussian War, "perfidious Albion" discarded the French-style chaco which the infantry had worn since the Crimea, and adopted a modified style of *Pickelhauber* which carried an even sharper brass spike. However, unlike their German counterparts, the British soldier of 1914 went into battle wearing a flat khaki cap.

Church parades, at which full dress was invariably worn before the Great War, posed a particular danger. A soldier could too easily place his helmet down on the pew and then sit on it, causing considerable mirth among his comrades, and exquisite pain to himself.

Hugo White, Bodmin, Cornwall

Who chooses the names for Royal Navy vessels?
Mike Smith, Falkirk

Names are chosen by the Ships Names and Badges Committee, four permanent members who include the Norroy and Ulster King of Arms, on a theme proposed by the First Sea Lord. This might be an initial, for example, A for the Amazon class of frigates, or place names, which usually encourages a degree of lobbying from interested cities and counties.

The committee, headed by Captain Chris Page, will consider suggestions from any quarter, but the final decision rests with the Queen. Recent proposals have included "HMS Death Star" and "HMS Millennium Falcon", which failed to make the shortlist and doubtless disappointed the 390,000 Jedi Knights reported in the last census.

Anyone wishing to suggest a name for a future Royal Navy ship is urged to write to:

The Chairman of the Ships Names and Badges Committee
(Head of the Naval Historic Branch)
3–5 Great Scotland Yard
Whitehall
London SW1A 2HW

Steve Hibbs, Newport, Gwent

From 1940 to 1942, corvettes from the Flower class were launched with names such as *Meadowsweet*, *Periwinkle*, *Wallflower*, *Rhododendrum* but not, with man-of-the-world delicacy, "Pansy".

Was this recorded by Nicholas Monsarrat, author of *The Cruel Sea*?
Michael Flynn, Chesterfield, Derbyshire

Contrary to your previous response, there was indeed a Flower class corvette named HMS *Pansy*, whose name was eventually changed to HMS *Heartsease* to spare matelots' blushes.

Incidentally, there is a flourishing Flower Class Corvette Association of veterans of these ships and their families, whose annual reunion takes place this weekend at Leamington Spa.

Helen Whiteley, Bushey, Hertfordshire

If it can be said that war has its lighter moments, then the Second World War service of His Majesty's dhows *Primrose* and *Cowpat* provided such a brief interlude.

The Senior Naval Officer Aden, in 1940, was Rear Admiral Murray, a seaman with much experience of the eccentricities to be found in life and in naval service.

One eccentric, with whom he had to deal, was Lt Cmdr Cardell-Ryan, a reserve officer from Ireland. Cardell-Ryan had aquired two Arab trading dhows which were pressed into service to carry Belhaven's long-range desert group. Ryan requested permission to fly the White Ensign from his command, "HMD" *Primrose* and "HMD" *Cowpat*, to be told by the senior naval officer that under no circumstances would such permission be granted.

Lord Belhaven, who was to carry out the penetration of Italian-occupied Somaliland and Ethiopia and for whom these vessels would be an ideal means of landing his group, became involved. He was present at a meeting between the Irish skipper and his admiral at which the former asked what flag he might fly and was told: "The skull and crossbones or any bloody flag you like as long as it is not the White Ensign."

John Bushell, Salisbury

There were patrol boats named HMS *Gay Bombardier* and *Gay Cavalier*, among others, in the "Gay class" of the 1950s. There was also a destroyer, HMS *Dainty* (1950).

Mind you, the names of the "24 Class" minesweepers of 1918–19 take some beating: HMS *Isinglass*, *Merry Hampton* and *Sir Visto* among them — all named after winners of the Derby. My favourite British warship names, however, are the "Dance class" of minesweepers of 1917–18. These included HM Ships *Fandango*, *Hornpipe*, *Morris Dance*, *Pirouette*, *Quadrille* and *Step Dance*.

Lester May, London NW1

It's not just the Royal Navy that has had some interesting ship names.

While the Australians have a frigate named HMAS *Newcastle*, the Royal Navy has a destroyer named HMS *Newcastle*. They're named after two different cities; it's just the cities that happen to share the same name. This has also happened with Britain and America. Both countries have had ships named *Manchester*, *Birmingham*, *Essex* and *Boston*, and for less obvious reasons, others named *Bristol* and *Fife*. Our ships were named after the cities, the American ones were named after US Navy Admirals Bristol and Fife.

Additionally, the Royal Navy once had a minesweeper named HMS *Spanker*.

James Hamblin, Hayes, Middlesex

Is it true that Old Boys of Stonyhurst College have won more VCs than those of any other school?

Christopher Bell, Sevenoaks, Kent

The college website records that Old Boys of Stonyhurst include seven VCs (as well as the great-grandfather of George Bush and a signatory to the American Declaration of Independence). Eton College numbers in excess of 20 VCs among its Old Boys and a few other schools match or surpass the record of Stonyhurst.

There is an area of distinction in which I should be surprised if Stonyhurst can be matched, however: the website also claims no less than 22 saints and martyrs as Old Boys of the college.

Nigel Platts, Sanderstead, Surrey

Kirby and Walsh have written a book about "The Seven VCs of Stonyhurst College" but whether this is a record remains in some doubt. For concentration of VCs per school population, though, Elizabeth College in Guernsey takes some equalling — four VCs from a school a fraction the size of Stonyhurst or Eton.

Sarah Cash, St Peter Port, Guernsey

Though Stonyhurst may not be able to boast the greatest number of VCs won by any one school I remember hearing that the college can claim to have had among its pupils the first recipients of the VC in both world wars.

Brian Austin, West Kirby

During the period 1979–2000, I was the commanding officer of the

Stonyhurst College Cadet Corps. The inquiry about the number of VCs awarded to Old Boys of the college compared with other schools was frequently raised and so led me to research the matter officially. I subsequently learnt that the medal had been awarded to former pupils of schools as follows:

Eton: 33
Harrow: 20
Wellington: 15
Cheltenham: 14
Marlborough: 12
Dulwich, Haileybury, Westminster and Stonyhurst: 7 each

Further to your last correspondent, Stonyhurst could *nearly* claim to have Old Boys who were the first to receive the Victoria Cross in both conflicts. Lieutenant Maurice James Dease, 4th Battalion, The Royal Fusiliers, was certainly the first recipient of the award in the First World War. A second Old Boy, Captain Harold Marcus Ervine-Andrews, the East Lancashire Regiment, was similarly decorated in the Second World War, with an announcement in the *London Gazette* of July 30, 1940 of his heroism in action on May 31-June 1, 1940 at Dunkirk. It was, however, 2nd Lieutenant Richard Wallace Annand (educated at Pocklington School, and who incidentally is still alive) who was the first to receive the VC in that conflict, although publication was not given until August 23, 1940. His individual heroism took place on May 15, 1940, near the River Dyle, Belgium.

John Cobb, Bolton-by-Bowland, Lancashire

Stonyhurst possibly has an eighth VC, namely General Sir Henry Hugh Clifford (born 1826), one of the original Inkerman VCs. While there were ten members of the Clifford family at Stonyhurst in the 1830s and 1840s, including a Charles Hugh and a Henry William, the college register does not show "Henry Hugh" — despite his own Crimea diaries referring to time spent at Stonyhurst. If any reader can shed further light on this matter, I believe that the college would be most interested.

Christopher Page, Cirencester, Gloucestershire

Major-General the Hon Sir Henry Clifford, VC, KCMG, CB, who won his VC for his gallantry at the Battle of Inkerman on November 5, 1854, was educated at Prior Park and the University of Fribourg.

The mention of Stonyhurst in the introduction to *Henry Clifford,*
VC, published in 1956 by my father Cuthbert Fitzherbert, a grandson
of the VC, appears to have been an error.
                    Nicholas Fitzherbert, Much Hadham, Hertfordshire

**During the First World War, what happened when the trench
system reached the Belgian coastline? Did the fortifications
extend into the sea for any distance? Were there any attempts by
either side to outflank the other in this way?**
                    Harry Spry-Leverton, Barrowden, Rutland [30/09/03]

The First World War trench lines ran from the Swiss border to the
Belgian coast at Nieuport, south of Ostend. In 1914 King Albert of
Belgium ordered the sea sluice-gates to be opened at Nieuport, flood-
ing the surrounding lowlands to deny access to the advancing German
Army. This area remained flooded and the trench lines diverged around
the flooded area, with the German Army holding the north and the
Belgians the south. Here, the front lines were a mile or more apart but
did literally extend down to the seashore.

In 1917 the original plan for the battle of Third Ypres, which became
known as Passchendaele, was for an outflanking attack up the coast to
clear the U-boat bases at Ostend and Bruges, with its outlet to the sea
at Zeebrugge. The British Army took over some of the line at Nieuport
in preparation but the German Army attacked first to prevent such a
move, leading to the little-heard-of Battle of the Nieuport Dunes in
the early summer of 1917. As a result that part of the plan was abandoned and Passchendaele became a battle to capture the high ridge of
ground northeast of Ypres, with resultant enormous losses to the
British and Empire Armies.

The Belgian coast was only finally cleared in the last 100 days of
the war when the German Army began its final retreat towards the
German borders.
          Christopher John, Birmingham Branch, Western Front Association,
                                                    Sutton Coldfield

My father, who served in the Manchester Regiment throughout the
war, used to say that on three occasions he commanded the extreme
left-hand post in the British frontline: in 1915 in Gallipoli, in 1916 in
Egypt facing the Turks from Palestine and in 1917 on the Western Front

in the Nieuport area, where he says "his left-hand machine-gun positions was lapped by the sea at high water".

As a child in 1938, I visited the last position: a pill-box in concrete. He did not mention ever being outflanked. The area in front had been extensively flooded in the war by breaching the sea defences and was difficult to cross.

Patrick Bryan, Cheltenham

In 1930 my parents took me on holiday to Ostend. One day we went by steam tram down to the border at Nieuport to look at the battlefield. Between the river and the remnants of the town was a large area of sand dunes, which we walked over, with the remains of heavy fighting on them. There was much rusty debris, bits of uniforms, old boots, spent cartridges, remnants of trenches and lots of barbed wire. I still have a cartridge case I picked up.

We were told that if we hired a guide, he could show us bones and boots with feet still in them. The town was still in ruins. In the towns there were temporary octagonal dioramas, which for a small fee you could walk around to see mock-ups of battle scenes.

We visited Zeebrugge Mole where the famous attempt at a seaborne attack took place. I was eight at the time and still have vivid memories of that exciting holiday.

Peter Blackwell, Sudbury, Suffolk

For some 200 years, the English annihilated armies (which sometimes outnumbered them 5–1) by use of the longbow. Why did opponents never cotton on to this obvious matchwinner and train their own archers?

W. Newbigging, Meols, Cheshire

The English adopted the Welsh longbow and turned it into a very effective weapon by using massed plunging fire against armoured soldiers. However, it was not quite as decisive a weapon as later English propaganda made out. The bow required considerable strength and skill to use, hence much initial training and continual practice. Even into the 17th century, the law in England required men to practise archery weekly. Scots Highlanders also adopted the longbow but they were never able to develop massed units as the English had. Some Italian city states hired mercenary English longbow companies rather than go through the difficult business of raising and maintaining their own.

The one state that made determined efforts to copy the English was France. Charles V (1364–80) decreed that all male subjects should train with the bow or crossbow, but rescinded the order under pressure from the nobles, who were alarmed at the prospect of an armed peasantry. Charles VII (1422–61) set up francs-archer companies by requiring every fiftieth household to train a bowman. The nobility mocked them with the nickname *francs-taupins* (moles) because of their practice of digging protective earthworks, and these troops proved poor in combat. By the time they were disbanded by Louis XI (1461–83) they were commonly ridiculed as "chicken killers". Louis reformed the francs-archer in 1466 as 28 companies each of 500 men armed with crossbows and arbalests, but they were disbanded for indiscipline and cowardice after the battle of Guinegate in 1479.

It was therefore, arguably, the distinctive English social system in medieval times that supported and made the longbow companies effective. In the 16th century, however, this resulted in the English clinging to the longbow as the main missile weapon long after it was rendered obsolete by improved firearms.

Russell Vallance, London SE16

Were there any pilots on either side who flew in action in both the First and Second World War?

Peter Gosling, Stamford, Lincolnshire

A significant number of senior pilots from the First World War served with Air rank or as instructors during the Second, and a few saw active service. The leading Belgian ace Willy Coppens de Houthulst, DSO (37 victories), was still flying with the Belgian Air Force when the German Army invaded in May 1940.

Captain J. Ira T. Jones, DSO, MC, DFC, & Bar (40 victories, 74 Squadron, RAF), was recalled to active service in August 1939 and participated unofficially in some fighter sweeps; he is also reputed to have attacked a Ju 88 in a Henley target tug, armed only with a signal pistol.

One definite action was that of Marius (Marc) Ambrogi, who served with Escadrille SPA.90 of the French Air Service in the First World

War, scoring 14 victories. He was demobilised in 1920, but flew again with the Groupe de Chasse 1/8 during the retreat of May 1940 and added a Ju 52 to his tally before his service finished at Toulouse.

Stephen Adams, Reading

As a flying instructor at No 7 EFTS, RAF Desford during the Second World War, I recall a fellow instructor who wore an RFC Brevet with a DFC ribbon below it.

Flight Lieutenant Nock seemed to me at the time to be quite an old man, although this was relative to my tender years. He was reluctant always to talk of his First World War experiences, but the DFC told its own story.

Dennis Berry (former Flight Lieutenant), New Malden, Surrey

Lieutenant-Colonel P. S. Joubert, DSO, AFC (my late husband's uncle by marriage), flew in the South African Air Force campaigns against German Colonies in South West and East Africa in 1915–16 and then transferred to the Royal Flying Corps.

In 1940 he was recommissioned in the SAAF and in 1943 was seconded to the Royal Air Force as a ferry pilot. At Down Ampney he was teased about his age, brown uniform and accent, but towed gliders from D-Day onwards to Arnhem and other destinations. He died in 1945, aged 49, in a firework accident on VJ Day.

Mrs D. F. G. Mosenthal, Richmond, Surrey

Louis Strange was a stunt and racing pilot before the First World War, and joined up and saw action as a fighter pilot, pioneering tactical bombing and ground attack in company with Lanoe Hawker, VC. He ended the war as a lieutenant-colonel, DSO, MC, DFC, commanding 80 Wing and was mentioned in dispatches three times. He was described by Smith Barry, who evolved the system of pilot training adopted by the RAF, as "the bravest man in the world".

He rejoined at the start of the Second World War. After pulling many strings, he was posted to flying duties and was involved in flying supplies to beleaguered British troops during the German invasion of France. Over Boulogne, he got into a scrap with some Messerschmitts, but managed to avoid them by flying down a village street, down the local château drive and, in his own words, "almost through the château door", and back to a safe landing at Manston. For all of this he was awarded a bar to his First World War DFC — one of only a few to receive the award in both wars.

Cecil Lewis was sent to France in early 1916 and was eventually selected by Albert Ball, VC, to join 56 Squadron. He finished the war with a Military Cross and eight victories. Earlier, with 44 Squadron, he was brought back to this country as part of the aerial defence against the German airship raids. His description of night flying with no training, no landing lights and no instrument illumination, is wondrous. In the Second World War, he rejoined and flew in Italy and Sicily.

Derek Gratze, Chelmsford, Essex

My father, Air Commodore J. W. B. Grigson, DSO, DFC, who died on active service in July 1943, joined the RNVR in 1913 and the Royal Naval Air Squadron in 1916. During the following five years, he saw service in the Eastern Mediterranean, the Caspian, South Russia, Egypt and Iraq, gaining a permanent commission in the RAF in 1918. Second World War service included postings in the UK, Egypt and Greece.

When he was presumed missing with HMS *India* in August 1915, a planned memorial service was hastily transformed into a service of thanksgiving, following the arrival of a telegram reading: "Interned in Norway, please send fishing gear!"

Simon Grigson, Herriard, Hampshire

In the First World War, Oberleutnant zur See Theodor Osterkamp, a German ace, shot down 32 aircraft and was awarded the Pour le Merit. In the Second World War he commanded Jagd Geschwader 51 and claimed six victories during the battle for France — three Hurricanes, a Spitfire, a Blenheim and a Fokker Gl. He was awarded the Knight's Cross of the Iron Cross in 1940 and died in 1975.

Oberleutnant Hasso von Wedel scored five victories in the First World War and flew during the Second World War. He was shot down during the Battle of Britain flying a Messerschmit 109 and was repatriated but died defending Berlin at the end of the war. Wolfram Frieherr von Richthofen, cousin of the Red Baron, shot down eight aircraft in the First World War and in the Second World War was awarded the Knight's Cross with Oak Leaves for leading his Stuka bomber group in combat in Poland, France and the Russian Front.

The Rev Frank Parkinson, Faringdon, Oxfordshire

One was Air Vice-Marshal John Astley Gray. He joined the Royal Naval

Air Service in 1917 and transferred to the RAF on its formation in April 1918. Flying DH9s out of Dunkirk, he participated in many raids on German positions in Belgium, and on the day after the St George's Day naval raid on Zeebrugge, he flew on a photographic mission to assess the damage. He was shot down and landed across the Dutch border, where he was taken prisoner.

He served continuously in the Air Force and in 1929 was posted to 55 Squadron of Bomber Command, stationed in Baghdad, where the main job was to prevent bandits from Saudi Arabia stealing sheep. In those days the RAF was the sole power controlling Iraq. In 1941 as station commander at Honington in Suffolk, and with the permission of his AOC, he took part in several missions flying as co-pilot. He took part in raids on Mannheim and also on Brest, where the target was the *Scharnhorst*.

Air Vice-Marshal Gray retired in 1954.

Terence Fisher, Soham, Suffolk

Air Chief Marshal Sir Leslie (Holly) Hollingsworth, who died in 1974, went to France in 1914 with his own motorcycle as a dispatch rider, and later flew as a pilot with the Royal Flying Corps. When this was transformed into the Royal Air Force he stayed in the service and had air rank in Bomber Command during the Second World War.

He would often fly on missions over Germany as a morale-booster at a time when we were suffering considerable casualties, changing his rank for the trip to wing commander so as to deprive the enemy of a coup if he had to bale out or was killed.

Roy Roebuck, London N1

Yes. Biggles.

Frances Anderson, Glasgow

Wartime archive footage shows German infantry wearing helmets designed to cover the larger part of the skull extending over and around the temples, side and back of the head. In contrast, British soldiers wore helmets more resembling up-turned soup dishes. To the uninformed eye this appears to offer less protection. Is this the case, and if so, why?

Dr Henry Devereaux, Whitehaven, Cumbria

Steel helmets — always "tin hats" to the British soldiers whose officers often called them "battle bowlers" — were introduced when the First

World War became static with opposing trenches on the Western front stretching from Switzerland to the North Sea. As a result, the most frequent wounds were to the head — either as soldiers peered across the sandbags at the enemy and were shot by rifle fire or were struck by shrapnel from shells bursting overhead.

The British "soup plate" helmet, introduced in late 1915, had the characteristic broad brim that was designed to protect the top of the head from enemy bullets and deflect shrapnel from the shoulders and upper body as it showered down from shells exploding above. It did both very effectively. The Germans, however, used the "coal scuttle" helmet, based on the armour of 16th-century Teutonic knights, which gave greater coverage to the sides of the face and the nape of the neck, especially in "open" action outside the protection of the trenches.

Postwar research showed that frontline Germans suffered greater numbers of body wounds from overhead shrapnel. In fact, German troops were aware of this difference at the time and a "soup plate" was much valued (and used) armour during shrapnel bombardments of their trenches.

The Second World War was much more fluid, but Britain and her imperial armies still stuck with the "soup plate", perhaps mistakenly in the absence of trench warfare on the First World War scale. The Germans, however, perfected the "coal scuttle" still further and there is no doubt that their pattern saved many serious wounds in the much more open battles.

By the late 1960s the British Army had shifted to a lightweight model made from Kevlar which gives greater protection to the neck and ears. The United States has adopted the old German "coal scuttle" style which it now calls "Fritz" helmets.

Until 1941 the US had used the old British-style "soup plates".

Stanley Blenkinsop, Macclesfield [06/01/04]

The traditional pattern British steel helmet (also used by the US Army from 1918 to 1942) originated in the First World War as protection, primarily, from overhead airbursts of shrapnel. The German *stahlhelm* of the same period, nicknamed the "coal scuttle helmet" by British soldiers, provided better protection to the sides of the head and neck, but was heavier and more restrictive to movement. It was also thought to hamper hearing, as it covered the ears.

The distinctive shapes continued into the Second World War. The

Canadians produced a helmet that was slightly deeper and more rounded than the British version and the Americans abandoned it altogether in 1942 in favour of the familiar GI "pot" helmet. British and British-equipped forces continued with the "soup plate" or "battle bowler" pattern. Reasons given for its retention were that is was more portable when being carried rather than being worn; that it required no modification to use with earphones; and that it aided identification in night fighting as it was distinctive from the shape of the German helmet.

Undoubtedly, though, sentiment and tradition played as much a part as the logic of head protection: the battle bowler was part of our uniform, the coal scuttle was part of theirs.

Russell Vallance, London SE16

The British design had the advantage of speed and cheapness of production. In the First World War, the Mk 1 British helmet was manufactured out of a single sheet of manganese alloy. The Americans were so impressed with its design and simplicity that they ordered 400,000 from Britain to kit out their "Doughboys".

The German helmet was made of steel and was based on ones used during the Middle Ages. The Americans later adopted a version of the German helmet which has progressed into the standard Nato helmet.

The good thing about the Mk 1 was that when the British Army was "marching on its stomach" a soldier could, if necessary, utilise the helmet as an emergency cooking or eating dish.

Paul Britland, Torquay

My wartime Royal Navy training included instruction in close combat. Approaching a German sentry from the rear, we were taught that in reaching over and grasping the leading edge of the helmet and jerking it back, the presence of the chinstrap and the deep curve of the back of the helmet would ensure the breaking of the neck.

By contrast, the British helmet was not susceptible to such a procedure, but its weight and hard edge made it a formidable striking weapon.

Ralph Hill, Bexhill-on-Sea, East Sussex

It has been suggested by some people that Italian aircraft and crews were involved in the Blitz. Is there any knowledge or evidence of this?

Keith Douglas, Solihull

The Corpo Aereo Italiano did indeed participate, albeit to somewhat minimal effect, in the Blitz, and its involvement is excellently summarised in the book *Martlesham Heath* by Gordon Kinsey.

On November 11, 1940, a formation of approximately 10 Fiat BR20 twin-engined bombers, escorted by 40 Fiat CR42 fighters, based along the Channel coast, had as its objective the harbour installations at Harwich, Essex. During the engagement, its formation was broken and all its bombs fell in the sea.

The RAF squadrons that intercepted were No 42 from Hornchurch, Essex, Nos 46 and 245 from North Weald, Essex, and No 257 from Martlesham Heath, Suffolk; 46 Squadron claimed two bombers and two fighters destroyed and two more fighters "probable"; 245 Squadron claimed one fighter "probable", and 257 Squadron five bombers and two fighters destroyed and one further bomber and three fighters damaged. All our aircraft returned safely.

One CR42 fighter, piloted by Salvatori Pictio, 23, made a forced landing on the beach at Orfordness, Suffolk. The aircraft exists to this day, and is in the RAF Museum at Hendon.

A BR20 bomber was chased inland, and eventually crashed in Tangham Forest, near RAF Woodbridge, Suffolk. Among its contents were found a bottle of champagne, a bottle of Chianti and a 5lb cheese — together with a cheese grater.

Robert Warner, Woodbridge, Suffolk

As a political gesture Mussolini instructed the Regio Aeronautica to form an Italian Air Corps (Corpo Aereo Italiano) intended to assist his German allies in the action which became known as the Battle of Britain. This was officially formed on September 10, 1940 with two bomber *stormi* (wings) equipped with the Fiat BR20M, one fighter wing equipped with the biplane Fiat CR42 and Fiat G50 monoplane fighters and a strategic reconnaissance *squadriglia* (flight) with the new Cant Z1007bis.

These units were based in Belgium from late September 1940 with operational flying ceasing the following January. Their contribution to the conflict was minimal, due mainly to inadequate combat training, fuel shortages and obsolescence, not to mention the poor weather conditions.

Operations were in fact limited to a few raids along the Kent coast, which proved ineffective, with higher-than-expected losses.

Peter Danby, Market Harborough, Leicestershire

I remember reading during the war some verses on the Italian Air Force's participation in the Blitz. I can recall only the opening lines: "Avanti! Avanti! 'Mid fumes of Chianti the vaunted armada took off in the breeze." Can anyone provide the missing verses?

Frank O'Hare, Penn, Buckinghamshire

Your last correspondent asks for the missing lines of the verse "Avanti! Avanti! 'Mid fumes of Chianti the vaunted armada took off in the breeze.". The opening lines were, I think: "Each bulging Caproni / Packed tight with polony / Ripe macaroni and parmesan cheese", and then "Avanti! . . ."

Capronis were rather tubby aircraft and thus suitable for such cargo.

M. S. Charity, Axminster, Devon

Did Lord Nelson and the Duke of Wellington ever meet?

Sydney Scott, Theydon Bois, Essex

Nelson met the future Duke of Wellington in a room of the Colonial Office, where they were both waiting to see Lord Castlereagh. Nelson had no idea that he was talking with somebody of any reputation or importance, although Wellington recognised Nelson. According to Wellington: "He [Nelson] entered at once into conversation with me, if I can call it conversation, for it was almost all on his side and all about himself and, in reality, a style so vain and so silly as to surprise and almost disgust me."

Nelson then left the room for a moment, apparently to find out who exactly he had been speaking with. When he came back, his manner was totally different.

Wellington continued: "His charlatan style had quite vanished . . . and certainly for the last half or three quarters of an hour, I don't know that I ever had a conversation that interested me more. I saw enough to be satisfied that he was really a very superior man; but certainly a more sudden or complete metamorphosis I never saw."

Dr Jonathan Bird, Esher, Surrey

2. SPEAK THE SAME LANGUAGE

What is the origin of the phrase "As the actress said to the bishop"? Who was the actress and who was the bishop?

Mike Dutson, Manchester

As far as it can be verified, there was no original actress or bishop. The phrase has its origins in the early part of the 20th century, when the word "actress" was sometimes used as a euphemism for prostitute. The phrase is used to accompany a saucy joke or a *double entendre*, and rests upon contrasting the presumed propriety and innocence of the bishop and the loose living and lax morals of the "actress". Thus it is the actress who utters the innuendo, or an innocent statement that could be interpreted as smutty.

The phrase came fully into popular use in the 1940s and by the 1950s had become a constant on the wireless.

Arthur Rowlands, Norwich

I too had wondered about the history of this phrase, so I am grateful to for Arthur Rowlands's explanation. However, in the past year or so I have increasingly heard the expression used in reverse: ie, "as the bishop said to the actress". Assuming that Mr Rowlands is correct in his exegesis, I am beginning wonder about shifts in perception of episcopal "propriety and innocence", as well as of theatrical ladies' status. *O mores, O tempores.*

Michael Knight, Geneva

The phrase should go "'long time, no see' as the actress said to the archdeacon". The moral being that toying with thespians had thwarted the venerable one's promotion to the episcopacy.

H. A. N. Hallam, Southwold, Suffolk

I first came across the expression in the "Saint" books by Leslie Charteris. In one of the very first, *Enter The Saint*, first published in 1930, for example: "'And now let's get down to business — as the bishop said to the actress,' murmured Simon . . ."

This would suggest that the phrase was in common usage by then — or, possibly, that it was invented by Leslie Charteris for his character.

David Albury, Edinburgh

Until the mid-18th century the letter "s" at the beginning and in the middle of words was represented by one similar to an "f". What was this letter called, was it pronounced "f" and why did it disappear?

Peter Bicknell, Thorncombe, Somerset

This was simply what is known as a "long s" — it is a similar curve, but drawn upwards. Originally, the short "s" was only used at the ends of words, and the long version elsewhere. In German, where there is a double "s" — in English, "ss" — at the ends of words, the double letter is represented by "ß", a symbol which is actually a long s with a short one attached. The long s was used on gravestones in our churchyard well into the 19th century, and can usually be distinguished from what is an "f" by the absence of a crossbar.

Mike Harries, Northwich, Cheshire

As to when it disappeared from the printed page, D. B. Updike writes in his monumental work on *Printing Types* that "The abolition of the long s, it is popularly thought, we owe to the London publisher John Bell, who in his *British Theatre*, issued about 1775, discarded it. Franklin, writing in 1786, says that "the Round s begins to be the Mode and in nice printing the Long f is rejected entirely". In fact its use continued for some years after these dates and the "long s" can still occasionally be found in works of the early 19th century, especially those executed by provincial printers.

Bruce Tice, Saffron Walden, Essex

This lasted much longer than the early 19th century. I have just received copies of entries in the Register of Births and Marriages for Edinburgh — where James Russell, Registrar, signed his name with a long S in 1890 and R. W. Charlton in 1892 used a long-s when writing "assist" against the printed word Registrar.

Michael J. Harte, Wadhurst, Sussex

I have always understood that the necessity for the use of "f" initially and in the middle of words arose when the New Testament was translated from the Greek. In Greek lower-case Sigma has two forms, the strong and the weak. The monks, striving for accuracy in their work, saw the resemblance of "f", when stripped of its cross-stroke, to a long and therefore weaker "s"; so they used that as a substitute.

Archie Thomson, Whitby

The long "s" appears to have remained in use in handwriting long after it was discarded by the printers. I have a postcard dated 1905 from my grandfather to his wife-to-be, on which the "Miss" of the address is written with the intermediate long "s" as the penultimate letter and the modern (finial) short "s" as the final letter — the result looking similar to the modern German ligature. He does not, however, use the long "s" elsewhere in the text, preferring the modern short "s" even in initial and intermediate positions. Unfortunately, there is no word in the text ending "ss", so I cannot tell whether the usage was his normal one or just a flourish for the address.

Michael J. B. Almond, Errol, Perthshire

The long "s" lives on in the integration sign "∫" ("sum") in mathematics. In connection with the origin of the pound sign in the old system of pounds, shillings and pence (l = libri, s = solidi, and d = denarii), the "l" was stylised into the symbol £, and the "s" into a straight slightly sloping line, as in £1–6/8d. This used to be called a solidus, but has become a more general divider nowadays called a slash.

Michael Harman, Camberley, Surrey

Why and when did newts acquire their reputation for inebriation?
Peter Hayes, Gloucester

One explanation suggests that the saying came to Britain in the Second World War from the US. In this instance, newt is a corruption of "Inuit". Due to their genetic make-up, Eskimos are allegedly more susceptible to alcohol than other races.

A second explanation goes back to the 18th century or so, when gentlemen spent much time in gaming houses. They left their horses outside in the care of young boys, whom they called "newts". They often sent these young lads a warm-up drink or two during the long evening, only to find them somewhat inebriated when they came to collect their horses.

Dr James Briggs, Bristol

The phrase is an anglicisation made when Cornish was no longer understood in most parts of England, perhaps in about the 13th century. The phrase will originally have been "os pyst os yn neweth". It simply means "Thou art daft, thou art in (second) childhood." Newts do not enter into it.

The Rev John L. V. Woods, Much Wenlock, Shropshire

My understanding is that the expression did indeed originate with GIs stationed in England during the Second World War. However, the expression was originally "As drunk as a Ute", after a tribe of North American Indians with a reputation for drunkenness. The locals here would not have known the world "Ute" and thought the expression was "As drunk as a newt".

Alan Kennedy, Radlett, Hertfordshire

I would offer another as to the origins of the saying. The author of a book on the medicinal properties of the beer of Burton-on-Trent was Abraham Newton (1631–98). He was well known for taking the odd beer, and locals coined the expression "drunk as Abe Newton". Over time this expression became corrupted to the one which is used today.

Richard Vernon, Ashford, Kent

Who was Roger and why was he jolly? Who was Larry and why was he happy?

Robert Randell, Sydenham, London

The term "Jolly Roger" is of course linked to the skull and crossbones of pirate ships. One of the first pirates to use this style of flag was the infamous Welsh pirate, Black Bart (Bartholemew Roberts, b. 1682 Haverfordwest). His flag depicted a skeleton with an hourglass. The rambunctious Black Bart wore red damask and velvet from head to toe, a three-cornered red hat with a huge scarlet plume and was armed with cutlasses and pistols. His demeanour was such that French traders called him *"Le Joli Rouge"*. This description eventually became linked with his flag, and it was only a matter of time before the flag became known as the "Jolly Roger".

Diz Williams, Prestatyn, Denbighshire

It is commonly held that the expression "happy as Larry" comes from Larry Foley, an Australian boxer who lived from 1847 to 1917. Apparently he was never defeated, retired as champion, made a good deal of money and lived to 70. He died, well, as happy as Larry.

Ian Paul, Poole, Dorset

Having explained why Roger was jolly and how Larry came to be so happy, can anyone explain why Riley was living the life of . . .

Mark Heywood, Croydon, Surrey

According to *Brewer's Dictionary of Phrase & Fable*, the allusion is said to be to a comic song, *Is that Mr. Reilly?* by Pat Rooney, which was popular in the USA in the 1880s. The hero fantasised about what he would do if he "struck it rich". However, its use has apparently not been recorded earlier than 1919, when it was popularised by the following:

Faith and my name is Kelly, Michael Kelly, But I'm living the life of Reilly just the same.

(H. Pease: *My Name is Kelly*.)

Gordon Brudenell, Sutton Coldfield

There is one distinct possibility that goes back to the era of the Victorian music hall. One of the popular songs of the time was about an Irishman named O'Reilly who dreamed of making a fortune and then leading a life of luxury. The song was called *Are you the O'Reilly* in which the audience joined in the chorus, ending up with the last line which was "Cor blimey, O'Reilly, you are looking well". My earliest certain reference to the actual phrase is in a 1919 song *My Name is Kelly*, clearly based on well-established usage.

Dr James Briggs, Bristol

The most likely explanation for the root of the expression lies in the translation of its meaning from the Irish. Reilly, or Riley, is an Anglicised version of Ragheallach which is *ragh*, meaning race, and *ceallach*, meaning gregarious. They obviously had a reputation for having a good time. The head of the O'Reilly clan was, until the 16th century, the Prince of East Brefny (Co. Cavan). After that the head, as with other Irish families, simply prefixed his name with the definite article, hence "The O'Reilly". They were wealthy and held large estates throughout Cavan, Meath, Louth and Down into the 20th century.

Patrick Pilkington, Coole, Co. Westmeath

Who were the original Tom, Dick and Harry, and what did they do to make them memorable?

Sue Duys, Draycott, Somerset

The phrase is an Anglicised corruption of the Cornish phrase "*an tamm diek or'n arja*", which means "the clod of a farmer at the plough". It is notable that the phrase retains its original deprecatory meaning.

The Rev John L. V. Woods, Much Wenlock, Shropshire

Here's what *Brewer* says: "Tom, Dick and Harry. A Victorian term for the 'man in the street', more particularly persons of no note; persons unworthy of notice. Brown, Jones and Robinson are for other men; they are the vulgar rich, who give themselves airs, especially abroad, and look with scorn on all foreign manners and customs which differ from their own."

Dr James Briggs, Bristol

Three brothers, Tom, Dick and Harry Dunsden, became notorious high-waymen around the Oxfordshire-Gloucestershire borders in the late 18th century. Their misdeeds and deaths formed a large part of local legend for the two centuries following their widely publicised exploits. Dick died first in an unpleasant encounter with lawkeepers; Tom and Harry were executed in Gloucester in July 1784 after a night of drunken gambling at the annual Whitsun Feast. After the execution, their bodies were brought back in a horse-drawn wagon over the Cotswolds to Capps Lodge on the Downs, and hung in chains on an oak tree, known as the Gibbet Tree.

Many people visited the tree that summer while the corpses were still there. The bodies were removed secretly in the autumn of 1784 and buried elsewhere but the chains were still to be seen in the 1930s.

Joan Moody, author, Burford's Roads and Rogues Part Two: Vagabonds, Villains and Highwaymen, *Burford, Oxfordshire*

Latin and German nouns have three genders: masculine, feminine and neuter. French nouns have two. Our nouns have none. Why?
Geoffrey E. Barlow, Stoke-on-Trent

We do indeed have gendered nouns in English, eg, boy/girl, man/woman, but it is the only language (at least the only Indo-European language) that does not use gender for purely syntactic purposes. That is masculine, feminine and neuter nouns must take masculine, feminine and neuter adjectives, pronouns and articles. This syntactic gendering existed in the base language of Indo-European, and is more prevalent in more archaic languages: English having evolved relatively recently does not use it.But this syntactic gendering does not create gender forms. Girl in German is neuter, and therefore also not gendered pairs as in man/woman, boy/girl, since it is not an inflectional category but simply divides the lexicon into classes that govern agreement and therefore can be seen as a classificatory feature.

The older a language, ie, the closer it remains to the Indo-European base, the more likely for there to be lots of declensional and conjugational forms. Today this archaism has led to difficulties with correcting various forms of gender bias built into these languages. In French this would involve more than just the non-problematic addition of new vocabulary but a change in the whole classificatory system involving morphology/gender.

Dave McGrath Wilkinson, Preston

Old English nouns did have three genders, but unlike Latin the gender was usually indicated not by the ending or the declension but by the agreement of a strong adjective or one of the demonstratives (the, this, that, these, those). When the inflections of the adjective were reduced to a single ending and demonstratives gained a fixed form, the support for grammatical gender was removed. When grammatical gender disappeared, it was simply the idea of sex that was the sole factor in determining the gender of English nouns. Thus woman, which was masculine in Old English (*wif-mann*), because the second element of the word was masculine, is now feminine on grounds of sex, not grammatical gender.

Adrian Room, Stamford, Lincolnshire

I should add that the "chen" in *Mädchen* (originally *Mägdchen* — little maid) means "little". While *die Mägd* is female, all words with the suffix "chen" are neuter in German.

Eva Crowe, Basingstoke, Hampshire

The gender of an English noun is determined by its meaning, not its form. Masculine gender denotes males, feminine females, neuter objects with no sex. To this may be added common gender words like parent, neighbour or child.

James Elliott, Shrewsbury

"As a result of Hastings, the Anglo-Saxon tongue, the speech of Alfred and Bede, was exiled from the hall and tower, from court and cloister, and was despised as a peasants' jargon, the talk of ignorant serfs. The learned and pedantic lost all interest in its forms. During these three centuries when our native language was a peasants' dialect, it lost its clumsy inflections and elaborated genders, and acquired the grace, suppleness and adaptability, which are among its chief merits." So wrote G. M. Trevelyan in his *History of England*.

Desmond Hartley, Windermere, Cumbria

Were the originators of Semitic scripts, those written from right to left, left-handed?

Christopher Brougham, London NW1

It is thought that Semitic scripts are written from right to left precisely because of the fact that their developers were right-handed. This is because one would hold a chisel in the left hand and the mallet in the right hand. Hence, the natural direction of progression of the writing would be to the left.

The first such alphabet was the so-called Proto-Sinaitic Script and this appeared around 3,800 years ago in the Sinai Desert. Greek was also originally written from right to left. Our word alphabet derives from the two words *aleph* and *beit*, which respectively mean ox and house. These are the names of the first two letters of the original Proto-Sinaitic alphabet and these letters were in fact pictorial versions of those two items.

Professor Lawrence Doctors, Sydney

I am asking for suggestions for a third person singular pronoun which applies to both genders. Sentences such as "If somebody . . . then he/she" are cumbersome.

Roland Morriss, Stokenchurch, Buckinghamshire

The concord problem is caused by the third person singular indefinite pronouns — everybody, anybody, somebody, nobody, etc — being gender-neutral, while the personal pronouns (eg, she, her, he, him) and possessive pronouns (hers, his) and possessive determiners (her, his) are gender-specific. The informal solution is to enhance the meaning of the third person plural gender-neutral forms (they, them, their, theirs) to enable them to fill the hiatus. Despite being semantically generic, the various forms involved keep the basic syntactic (subject-verb) number agreement: "I assume everyone has brought their brain with them today — haven't they?"

This is the solution adopted by the majority of native English speakers. After all, the *OED*'s first quotation illustrating "they" used in this sense is from the 16th century. Incidentally, while "they" excludes the speaker, the pronouns "one" and "you" used in a generic sense include him/her.

Martin Murrell, Rayleigh, Essex

William Caxton wrote in the 15th century, "Each of them should make themself ready" and Shakespeare prayed that "God send everyone their heart's desire." Even British Telecom will inform you when you phone 1471 that "the caller did not leave their number." As we therefore already have a perfectly good way of saying "he/she", it seems pointless looking for a new and artificial alternative form.

Nicholas Pritchard, Southampton

All that is needed is to widen our existing usage of "it" — already used straightforwardly when the noun intended is "child", and in literature used by Mr. Mantalini with all due fondness when referring to his wife.

Anthony C. Davis, Harrogate, North Yorkshire

A. A. Milne, in the introduction to his *Christopher Robin Birthday Book* (1930), made a suggestion: "If the English Language had been properly organised . . . then there would be a word which meant both 'he' and 'she', and I could write, 'If John or Mary comes, heesh will want to play tennis', which would save a lot of trouble". I don't see "heesh" catching on; there is more hope for "s/he".

Kathleen McCullough, Winchester, Hampshire

The avoidance of misuse of the plural "they" can be nicely coped with recourse to neglected applications of single-letter words: thus we would have "I", "U", and "E", with he and she when gender needed identification. For the accusative I'd recommend "erm", with him or her when specifically needed. I haven't decided on the right word in this sense for his/her — "hes"?

Alan Long, Greenford, Middlesex

Could we not go back to the use of "one"?

D. J. Hutson, Ascot, Berkshire

Where does "quid", the slang word for pounds sterling, come from?

Peter Taylorson, Enfield, Middlesex

The "quid" was originally aristocratic schoolboy slang in late-17th-century England and referred to a guinea, not a pound. This was because the deals gentlemen made when gambling, or purchasing art or horses were in guineas. Among men brought up with the classics such a standard item of currency could be regarded as a *quid pro quo* — something to be exchanged for something else.

By the mid 19th century the word had filtered through the middle down to the lower classes, whose only knowledge of money in such amounts was in terms of the pound. Nonetheless, it is because of its Latin origin (*quid pro quo* literally means "a whit for which") that — other than in late-20th-century slang extensions such as "quids in" — it has no plural.

Mike Darton, Preston St Mary, Suffolk

How much space is needed for one to be able comfortably to swing a cat, and when did this become the standard measurement of room size?

John-James A. Hallissey, Luton

The phrase arose in the Royal Navy in the days of the "wooden walls". If a seaman required punishment it would normally be administered by tying him over a gun barrel — this was called "kissing the gunner's daughter" — and whacking him with a rope's end. This was performed on the gun deck where the headroom was normally about 4ft 6in. If it was a grosser offence the seaman might be sentenced to a flogging with the cat-o'-nine-tails, in which case it was carried out on deck, as there was not room on the gundeck to swing a "cat".

Archie Thomson, Whitby, North Yorkshire

The expression is found in Tobias Smollett's Humphry Clinker (1771). The Scottish novelist's protagonist here is distinguishing between the delights of the country and the discomforts of London:

"At Brambleton-hall, I have elbow-room within doors, and breathe a clear, elastic, salutary air — I enjoy refreshing sleep, which is never disturbed by horrid noise." But in London: "I am pent up in frowzy lodgings, where there is not room enough to swing a cat; and I breathe

the steams of endless putrefaction; and these would, undoubtedly, produce a pestilence, if they were not qualified by the gross acid of sea-coal."

It is generally held that Smollett, who went to sea as a ship's surgeon, is referring to the cat-o'-nine-tails.

Louis Stott, Aberfoyle, Stirlingshire

The questioner is quite capable of answering this himself. I am afraid that this epitomises the sad lack of interest in the experimental sciences that is found all too frequently in today's young people.

Ronald Turner, Southampton

The cat-o'-nine-tails was not invented until the mid-1600s, yet this expression was in use by the 1500s. It may be that the saying truly involves felines, since there used to be a "sport" of using swinging cats as targets for archers. This was either by their tails, in a sack, or in a leather bottle. Shakespeare's Benedick, in *Much Ado About Nothing* (Act I, Scene I), says "hang me in a bottle like a cat, and shoot at me".

Dr James Briggs, Bristol

Until the early 20th century, Latin in schools and universities was pronounced as if it were written in English. When did this practice begin and why? Was it an Anglican reaction to the Latin of the Roman Catholic Church?

Hugh Livesey, Taunton, Somerset

A definitive answer can be found in *Latin in Church: The history of its pronunciation*, by F. Brittain (2nd ed, 1955). The writer showed (i) that the pronunciation of ecclesiastical Latin throughout the ages has not differed essentially from the pronunciation of secular Latin; (ii) that Latin, both ecclesiastical and secular, has normally been pronounced in each country (including England) on the same principles as the vernacular; (iii) that the Reformation of the 16th century caused no change in the pronunciation of Latin, either ecclesiastical or secular.

He produced evidence that the old established Roman Catholic families in England opposed the introduction of the Italian pronunciation in the later 19th century. While everyone agreees that the "Reformed Classical" pronunciation introduced in the early 20th century is unsuited for singing, he argued strongly that much liturgical music, such as Masses, written by English composers, was written for, and would be far better sung in, the old English pronunciation rather than the modern Italian pronunciation.

The Rev John Pratt, Tiptree, Essex

From the early centuries AD, Latin came to be spoken with different accents throughout the Empire. There was no standard pronunciation, even in the Roman Catholic Church, but in the early 20th century Pope Pius X put pressure on national Roman Catholics Churches to go Italianate. This gradually won the struggle against national pronunciations.

Catholics in England (and in exile on the Continent) had always used the traditional English pronunciation. But from the 1840s, the flood of Anglo Catholic converts brought with them a love of imitating all things Roman, including Italianate Latin. However, the "traditional Catholics", including Benedictines and Jesuits, kept close to the English Latin they had used during their years of oppression or exile. Meanwhile, Anglicans continued to use English Latin in schools and lawcourts; in church it came into titles like Te Deum or Benedicite.

A further complication is that for hundreds of years there were also academic attempts in England, France and Germany to get back to a restored Classical pronunciation, partly so that Latin speakers could all understand each other. This Latin came to be used in most universities by the early 20th century, and it differs from the usage of the Roman Catholic Church , whose services are now mostly in the vernacular.

Harold Copeman, Oxford

When Churchill visited his old school at Harrow in 1941, he spent 20 minutes chatting to the three senior boys who were privileged to be introduced to him. Hearing that I was in the Classical Sixth Form, he asked what pronounciation of Latin we were taught. I said it was what we called the "new". He strongly disapproved. He claimed to have recently mocked a legal MP in the House of Commons who had used the phrase *de jure* pronounced "day yeury".

"I told him I hoped there were enough yudges to deal with his yuries," he chortled.

Brian Straton-Ferrier, Surbiton, Surrey

Both my parents were born in 1901. My father was taught the old method, my mother the new. As a student in the 1950s, I was with a group in Austria and was forced at one point to use Latin when with a group of Austrian students. We were reduced to writing it as they could not understand our Latin spoken "with an English accent" while we could not distinguish theirs from German.

Jill Jackson, Surbiton, Surrey

In the English language, we say that cats go "miaow" and dogs go "woof". What noises do animals make in other languages?

Alex Miller, Dorset

In Ancient Egypt the words for cat and dog were the onomatopoeic *miu* and *iuiu* respectively.

Martin R. Davies, Bristol

The Spanish equivalent of "cock-a-doodle-doo" is *kikiriki* and "woof" is *guau*.

Maureen Robinson, Belfast

When I was working in Xinjiang some years ago, in my efforts to learn Mandarin, I discovered in a child's school primer that Chinese dogs are described as barking: *wang! wang!*

Tom Donachie, Chesterfield, Derbyshire

French-speaking ducks say *coin-coin*, while in Spanish they say *cuá cuá*. French donkeys say *hi-han* and their turkeys say *glou glou*.

Kath Eadon, Sheffield

In the Korean and Japanese languages, dogs and cats cry *mong-mong* and *wan-wan* respectively.

Philip Martin, Braintree, Essex

In Sanskrit, a cow's lowing after its calf is represented, curiously, as *hing*.

Martin West, Oxford

Hungarian dogs go *vau*, the cats *miau*.

Peter Kaldor, Horsell, Surrey

The Thai equivalent of "cock-a-doodle-doo" is *eggi-eggai*.
Edward Simpson, Ware, Hertfordshire

My own cat says *mrkgnao*, but I suspect her of reading a lot of Joyce. Italian dogs go *baau baau*, a German dog will greet you with *wau wau*, and French ones are deemed to go *wouah wouah*. But animals are far better linguists than we are: if you go abroad they will speak to you in perfect English.
Nigel Forde, Pocklington, East Yorkshire

The correspondence sends me back to Aristophanes' comedy *The Wasps*, produced at Athens in 422 BC, in which a dog's bark is represented (line 903) as *hau hau* (pronounced "how how"). Both Aristophanes and other writers represent the cry of the sheep as *be*, with the long open Greek "e", not as in English "be".
Robin Birch, Oxford

My pupils are always amused to learn the noises that animals used to make in Latin: a horse — *hinnivit*; a dog — *latravit*; a cow — *mugivit*; a lamb — *balavit*.
David Elkington, Wellington, Somerset

The problem of words for animal noises is solved neatly in Esperanto by a single word, *bleki*, meaning "to make the sound of that animal". *La bovino blekis* — the cow moo-ed; *la hundo blekas* — the dog barks; *la anasoj blekos* — the ducks will quack.
   If needed for clarification, the type of animal can be put in front — *Mi audis cevalbleko* — I heard a neigh. Or to translate the two quoted, *katbleko* and *hundbleko*.
Geoff Hammerton, Derby

In Romanian, ducks go *mac, mac*; woodpeckers go *cioc, cioc* (pronounced "choc, choc"); cats go *mieu, mieu*.
Adrian Penna, Durham

My Japanese wife insists that cats say *niao* — or *goro-goro* when they purr. Pigs, however, say *boo boo* in Japan.
Nigel Meek, Marlow, Buckinghamshire

Polish dogs bark *hau hau*, pronounced in English: "how! how!"

(Nothing to do with the Polish football team's performance in the World Cup.)

Piotr Miklasinski, Walsall

Why do the Scots object to the adjective "Scotch" as in "Scotchman"? And when did they begin to object to it?
Tony Gray, Walsall

Perhaps the following rule might help: in general terms Scots or Scottish should be used. The term "Scotch" is usually applied to things that can be bought and sold, eg, Scotch beef, lamb, tomatoes, politicians etc.

Hugh Barr, Glasgow

I am in the process of transcribing hundreds of family letters written between the 1870s and 1900 by my great-grandmother (widow of a Free Church Minister in Edinburgh) and her family, to my grandfather, who was a medical missionary in China. Never once have I come across the word "Scottish" when describing someone or something from Scotland — "Scotch" is always used.

Frances Clemmow, Sandy, Bedfordshire

Pilgrims who have made the trip to Alloway, near Ayr, birthplace of the great poet Rabbie Burns, will have discovered that in the museum there, Burns used the word Scotch exclusively in his writings. Scotch was in general use up to the 1930s but later regarded as not being politically correct.

Geoff Townsend, Stoke-on-Trent

It is not clear why they do (and some few still don't). Possibly they associated it with their favourite tipple and its derivatives of excess and guilt. The objection would seldom have pre-dated the 20th century. Many educated people of my generation (I am an ancient) stick to their guns and still prefer to use Scotch and Scotchman. Sadly, during its steady obsolescence there was an element of U and non-U involved. Nancy Mitford records: "I have a game I play with all printers. I write Scotch, it appears in the proofs as Scottish. I correct it back to Scotch. About once in three times I get away with it." (Ed, *Noblesse Oblige*, 1956).

The word was preferred by the majority of distinguished Scotch writers — Scott, Hume, Carlyle, Stevenson, *et al*, and the country's greatest politician, Gladstone, among them. Perhaps it is not too late to revive what is old, tried and good: for, in Dr Johnson's familiar words, "Much may be made of a Scotchman if he be *caught* young."

Michael Kidson, Westonbirt, Gloucestershire

In response to your replies, notably all from English addresses, may I assert the position that I am a *Scotsman* or person of *Scottish* extract, being born in *Scotland*. I have always objected to the term "Scotch" in relation to my origins as this should only be associated with our national drink. Anything else that is termed "Scotch" is a misnomer and only detracts from that amber nectar. I would be interested in the reaction of the English if they were called after their national drink, namely "Teamen".

W. Lawson, Darvel, Ayrshire

We call them Eyeties, Frogs and Jerries. What do our European friends call us?

J. Leeming, Larbert, Stirlingshire

When I lived in Germany about 45 years ago I was told I was *Ausschuss*, a "Reject", as the Germans had expelled the Saxons some 1,500 years ago.

David Fellows, Crowborough, East Sussex

To our German friends, we British are simply known as *Insel Affen*, or Island Apes.

Roger Dodson, Barnstable, Surrey

The French call the English *les rosbifs*. I would also continue the gastronomic flavour of this question by suggesting that the English refer to the Germans more often as Krauts rather than Jerries. I have never actually heard anyone use the term "Jerries".

Simon Dalgleish, London W6

In France you are called *bifteques* or *godons*. The term *godons* goes back to the Hundred Years War when the English soldiers were heard swearing at Agincourt: "goddam".

Michelle O'Gorman, Chelmsford, Essex

Poles call the English "jam eaters".

Piotr Miklasinski, Walsall

Since the person who posed the question comes from Stirlingshire, the answer is of course: "Scotch" (and not "Scottish").

Susan Persaud, Stoke-on-Trent

If your correspondent regularly refers to the Italians, French and Germans as Eyeties, Frogs and Jerries he deserves to be called whatever rude names they can think of in their respective languages.

Such racism is quite disgraceful.

Fen Crosbie, Edinburgh

Some French friends enjoyed writing a small "*de*" between the letters of my English friend's GB car sticker. This refers to the expression "*gueules de bois*", referring to a hangover or headache. Other friends living in northern France referred to those coarse "booze-cruise" Calais daytrippers, less favourably, but perceptively, as "*les f—offs*".

Pete Bull, Nottingham

Did "Disgusted of Tunbridge Wells" ever really write to newspapers?

Michael Hammerson, London N6

"Disgusted of Tunbridge Wells" was a character invented by Frank Muir and Denis Norden and played by Wallas Eaton in the hugely popular *Take It from Here* BBC Radio comedy of the 1940s and 1950s.

Roger Ordish, Lewes, East Sussex

"Disgusted: Tunbridge Wells" goes back to the well-known radio comedian Richard ("Dickie") Murdoch who once lived in the town. The joke was used frequently in the long-running radio show *Much Binding in the Marsh*, which co-starred Kenneth Horne and which was, in its day, almost as popular as *ITMA*.

Robert Hardcastle, Tunbridge Wells

Although nobody actually signs "Disgusted of Tunbridge Wells", the vitriol contained in letters to the local paper seems to suggest that the burghers of this town are easily disgusted: by the lack of public toilets and by the way in which the council collects refuse. I am disgusted to be associated with them.

Ben Cackett, Tunbridge Wells

Why are there so many words — enough to preclude coincidence — in French that start with "e" when the Latin base begins with "s"? This can even be seen in English words: space, spice, school, spinach, state, Spain . . .

Joseph Logue, Boston, Massachusetts

The extraneous initial "e" before s+consonant occurs not only in French, but in Spanish and Portuguese. The original speakers of these languages were Celts who adopted Latin. Most Celtic languages do not tolerate s+consonant at the beginning of a word. This is still true of modern Welsh (school, for example, is *ysgol*). When the Celts adopted Latin they retained this Celtic feature. Italian, on the other hand, whose original speakers were Latins, has no such objection, as in *spaghetti*, *scusi* and *stazione*.

Mike Day, Criccieth, Gwynedd

In many instances in French the "e" has gained importance and the "s" has disappeared: *école, état, épinards*. In Spanish and Portuguese, however, the "s" has remained: *escuela, espinacas* (Spanish), *escola, espinafre* (Portuguese), *estado* (both).

The Italians didn't encounter the same problem with pronunciation. Although initial "di" and "de" in words of Latin origin, such as "discover" and "descend", remain in French, Spanish and Portuguese, they have disappeared in Italian, leaving *scoprire* and *scendere*.

Jessie McKeown, London E15

Most of the French cognates that exist in the English language came into the language from Norman French. At that time, words that we recognise today as *épice, école* and *état* would have been spelt "*espice*", "*escole*" and "*estat*" — the absent "s" being denoted by the acute accent on the "e" in modern French. It appears that following the absorption of such words into what became the English language, the "e" from each word was dropped through a process of contraction, rather as the "s" disappeared from the words on the other side of the Channel.

This can also be seen in *hôtel* and *côte*, where the circumflex indicates where an "s" used to be in medieval French, throwing up into English "hostel" and "coast".

Gareth Williams, Gloucester

Mike Day is not absolutely correct in his analysis that most Celtic languages do not support s+consonant at the beginning of a word. Take "write" for example. The original Latin word was *scribere* (*scrivere*). This transmuted into *escire* in Old French, *yscrifo* in Welsh, and, incidentally, *yscrive* in Anglo Saxon. However, all the Brythonic languages other than Welsh supported s+plus consonant, ie, Cornish (*scryva*) and Breton (*skrivan*), as did all the Goidelic languages, ie, Irish and Scots Gaelic (*scriobh*) and Manx (*screeu*).

Ralph Watmough, St Cosme en Vairais, France

Why do some situations, usually of a sinister or tragic nature, occur in "broad" daylight?

Peter Sutherland, London W2

For the same reason that surprising revelations of a sexual nature are made on "national" television and police who don't know what they are looking for seek "vital" clues, often using "fingertip" searches.

George Middleton, Swinton, South Yorkshire

Although it is superficially tempting to look at the modern German cognate *breit*, and suggest an original meaning of "bright daylight", this has to be rejected owing to the date of the appearance of the phrase, which is at least 14th-century in its origins.

Though the Old English/Anglo-Saxon "brad" had essentially the same meaning as our modern derivative, namely "wide, expansive", there derived from this a secondary meaning of "abundant" (the *Beowulf* poet can talk of "broad gold" when he means that there was a large amount of it). This may originally have been for purposes of poetic alliteration, but passed into ordinary usage at an early stage. "Broad" daylight is therefore a time when light is abundant, full day — not half-light.

Karl Wittwer, The English Companions, London WC1

Although this expression may be peculiar to the English language, the stylistic idea of the expression is not. For example, in Bulgarian, dark deeds are done "in the middle of a white day", the connotation of "white" being "clear and innocent".

The expression obviously aims to emphasise the tragic nature of the event in a twofold way. The first implication is that while such crimes are usually carried out under the cover of darkness, the perpetrators on this occassion were so ruthless and desperate that they struck in the middle of the day. The second implication is that everyone could see it done but no one did anything about it.

Tchavadar Todorov, Belfast

When and why in English did we cease to use the second person singular — and did it have the same connotations as *tu* does to *vous* in French?

John Annesley, Storrington, West Sussex

In the earliest period of English the distinction between "thou" and "ye" was simply one of number, with thou the singular and ye the plural. In the 13th century, however, the singular forms (thou, thy, thee) came to be used among familiars and in addressing children or persons of lower social status, while the plural forms (ye, your, you) began to be used as a mark of respect in addressing a superior. This practice seems to have been introduced from French court circles. The usage then spread as a concession to courtesy until ye, your and you became the usual personal pronoun of direct address for everyone. By the 16th century, the singular forms had all but disappeared.

Adrian Room, Stamford, Lincolnshire

Until recently, I gave a lift every Friday to a Gloucestershire man born in 1916. He always greeted me with "Noice t' zither", which I interpreted as "nice to see thee". After inquiring what I had done that busy week, he would say: "Thee needs thy bloody head felt."

And how about Yorkshire's pithy: "Don't thee 'thou' me. Thee save thy thous for those that 'thou' thee." I'd say there is a *tu/vous* implication in that.

Muriel Brooks, Stroud, Gloucestershire

The second person singular (thou in the subjective, thee in the objective forms) seems to have dropped out of use in formal standard English and in some dialects of colloquial English at about the end of the 17th century. The development is best illustrated by transcripts of court hearings, which are almost the only verbatim records surviving from pre-technical times. For instance, in 1733 we read in Proceedings at the Sessions of the Peace (London) in the trial of a ship's cook for theft, the accused is addressed:

Court: "And how came you to Angel court?"

Whereas in legal proceedings almost 50 years earlier, Judge Jeffries contemptuously thees and thous a defendant, who must call him "you":

Jeffries: "Dost thou imagine that any man hereabouts is so weak as to believe thee?"

Dunne: "Tell me what you would have me to say."

The usage closely paralleled that of those modern languages which have a familiar and a deferential form of address. Children, animals and intimates are familiars: strangers and superiors are entitled to deference. God is always a familiar, and hence thee/thou in the *Book of Common Prayer* (and *tu* and *tú* in French and Spanish prayers). Tact for the dignity of inferiors was most probably what led to the loss of the singular form.

The connotations of the idiom are made clear by a passage from Sir Walter Raleigh's trial in 1603:

Prosecutor: ". . . that viper — for I thou thee, thou traitor."

Raleigh: "It becometh not a man of quality and virtue to call me so. But I take comfort in it, it is all you can do."

Thee and thou (hereabouts pronounced tha) are not quite dead, at least in some parts of Yorkshire. When I was a young man (40 years ago) the use was even more common. Only a few years ago, a Doncaster schoolboy addressed me as thee. This was clear insolence, and I replied with the Yorkshire put-down: "Sithee lad, thee tha them as thas thee, and not otherwise."

Michael S. Bruce, Selby, Yorkshire

The second person singular is still in daily use in the towns and villages of what was the Durham coalfield, and is used by young and old alike. As a child in the 1950s I remember miners using it in their dialect, and it has passed through the generations. For example: "Is that thine?" and "Is thou gannin yem?" ("Are you going home?").

Geoff Carr, Darlington

The Quakers use a form of the second person singular but a most peculiar one with, for example, "thee has" (accusative pronoun, 3rd-person singular verb) instead of "thou hast" (nominative pronoun, 2nd-person singular verb). But maybe we can't complain about that: standard English has lost nominative "ye" in favour of accusative "you".

David Joslin, Middlesbrough

In the late 1960s my Sheffield landlady used "thee" to her budgie, who knew he wasn't supposed to knock over the little ornaments on her mantelpiece but did it anyway. "What's tha' doing?" she would exclaim. "Tha' little booger!" (But she loved him dearly.)

Liz Young, Kingston-upon-Thames, Surrey

In a *Times* third leader last week the quotation "cometh the hour cometh the man" was used. I have busted a gut unsuccessfully searching for its provenance. Who said it?

Dorothy Wood, Exeter

I cannot guarantee the origin of the phrase, but Sir Walter Scott's *The Heart of Midlothian* (1818) begins an early chapter with:

> The hour's come, but not the man.
>
> There is a tradition, that while a little stream was swollen into a torrent by recent showers, the discontented voice of the Water Spirit was heard to pronounce these words. At the same moment a man, urged on by his fate, or, in Scottish language, fey, arrived at a gallop, and prepared to cross the water. No remonstrance from the bystanders was of power to stop him — he plunged into the stream, and perished.

The "cometh the man" expression is now, of course, generally used in a different sense.

Ray Chidell, Haywards Heath, West Sussex [03/12/02]

A variation of this expression was recorded by the 19th-century Cromarty polymath Hugh Miller (1802–56): "the hour has come but not the man".

He recorded the legend of a kelpie appearing in a false ford in the River Conon and uttering the expression. Kelpies would lure the unwary to their doom, so the local men who heard the utterance stopped an approaching rider from attempting to cross the river. For his own safety, the rider was locked in the local chapel but was later found to have drowned in the font.

Alan R. MacKenzie, Inverness

The American Confederate politician, William Yancey (1814–63), said of Jefferson Davis, President-elect of the Confederacy in 1861: "The man and the hour have met."

David Barron, Chipping Norton, Oxfordshire

The three examples published all post-date "You come most carefully upon your hour", from *Hamlet*, Act 1, Scene 1. Surely this is the origin.

Alan Mackesy, Cinderford, Gloucestershire

The phrase dates back to December 1948, and phonetically should be written: "coometh the hour, coometh the man". The scene is a Test Match, England versus South Africa, in the 1948–49 series, in Durban. England, batting last, needed only two or three runs to win with just one wicket remaining. Cliff Gladwin, the Derbyshire fast bowler and not much of a batsman, was the last man in, and as he made his way to the wicket, uttered the phrase in his broad Derbyshire dialect to his colleague, Alec Bedser, at the other end. England won the match, which is perhaps why the phrase is now part of cricket history.

Michael Barry, Taunton

Your last correspondent repeats a mistake made at the time of the 1948 Durban Test by someone in the media. Cliff Gladwin was alleged to have commented: "Coometh t'hour, coometh t'man", but a few years later I heard Gladwin himself reminiscing about the match and he was quite clear that his actual words had been: "When the hour cometh, so doth the man."

Incidentally, he was quite a decent batsman. He and the wicket-keeper, George Dawkes, rescued Derbyshire several times after one of their not infrequent batting collapses.

Francis Wetton, Cheadle Hulme, Cheshire

I always understood that this was the English form of the Latin saying "*hora dat vir*", literally, "the hour gives the man", and is therefore much older than previous correspondents have suggested.

Hugh Weatherly, Colchester

Why do we, the British, pronounce the word lieutenant as "leftenant". The Americans say "lootenant", which is surely correct, given the French root?

Michael Clewett, Polegate, East Sussex

Before the introduction of the printing press, almost all documents were either legal or ecclesiastical, and were written by hand in Latin or Anglo-Norman by scribes who were not always well educated or capable of writing perfectly clearly. The letter "u" was often written as "v" in these documents. What's more, the English tended to pronounce words as they saw them.

The sound of "v" and "f" are often barely distinguishable. Lieutenant would have become "lievtenat", then "lieftenant". The "i", being in a weak position, would have dropped out quickly — leaving "leftenant".

As for the American pronunciation which is nearer to the French, this can be accounted for by the strong influence of the language of the French colonists and the French Army in North America in the late 18th and early 19th centuries.

Eileen McGrane Morrison, Pelsall, West Midlands

Although frequently averred, the theory that the British pronunciation of "leftenant" is based upon a misreading of "v" for "u" in medieval manuscripts has to be rejected in face of the evidence. The forms "luftenant" and "leeftenant" are attested as early as 1375 and 1387 respectively.

"Lieutenant" derives ultimately from the Latin "*locum tenens*", that is, one who temporarily holds the place of a superior. In passing to its present French form, this seems to have gone through a stage where the case ending of the Latin was dropped (along the lines of "*loc' tenens*"), with the -c' here representing a gutteral, throaty noise something like the -*ch* of Scottish "loch".

In later French, this became a "labial glide" — *ieu*. In English, the guttural sound came to be pronounced as -*f* (as it also was in "cough") — though the spelling eventually came to follow the French.

Karl Wittwer, The English Companions, London WC1

When I was commissioned into the Royal Engineers in 1952, we were always addressed as "mister".

The pronunciation "leftenant" was considered a distinct solecism. The approved pronunciation was "l'tenant".

Kenneth Rubens, London NW8

Is there a term for the repetition of the last letter of an acronym as a whole word, such as "PIN number" or "ITN news"? This appears to be an increasingly common (annoying) habit.

Peter Bowen-Simpkins, Swansea

A term to denote such phrases could be AP — "acronymic pleonasm", or, less politely, PR — "pointless redundancy". Another awful example is "Lloyds TSB Bank".

Martin Murrell, Rayleigh, Essex

I have come across something similar in France — "*l'IRA irlandaise*" — which means "the Irish Irish Republican Army".

Maureen Robinson, Belfast

My father, a London taxi driver for 52 years, always said that any man who asked to be driven to "the RAC club" was clearly not a member.

Michael Cole, London SW7

It's called RAS syndrome; RAS stands for "redundant acronym syndrome". There is also "redundant RAS syndrome", one example of which is "human HIV virus".

John Grant, Cambridge

The opposite phenomenon to the "redundant acronym" is the "incorporated" or "absorbed" acronym, where the initial letter of one acronym is used in the construction of another. The World Meteorological Organisation (WMO) made use of this in the 1970s when the Global Atmospheric Research Program (GARP) spawned GATE, the Garp Atlantic Tropical Experiment.

WMO also managed to combine both the absorbed and redundant acronyms when they devised FGGE (pronounced "figgy"), the First Garp Global Experiment. I suggest this might be termed the "Absorbed Redundant RAS" or "ARRAS".

Tony Graeme, Sheep St, Charlbury, Oxfordshire

Just as intriguing as the possible term for the repetition of the last letter of an acronym as a whole word is the term for a missing whole word: "I'm taking my car for its MoT". Any suggestions?

Steve Ward, Bristol

The Ancient Egyptians often drew a picture after a word to help to explain its meaning. As modern acronyms have much of the obscurity of Egyptian hieroglyphs, repetition of part of the acronym in plain English helps in the same way.

Nothing like progress!

Dr Trefor Vaughan, Little Chalfont, Buckinghamshire

A carpenter is known as a "chippie", an electrician is known as a "sparky". What is a plumber also known as?

Robert Davis, South Molton, Devon

During my years in the building trade it was invariably "a drip".

Ian Trickett, Worthing, West Sussex

From having dealt with every kind of tradesman over the years, the plumber, in my experience, has always been referred to simply as a "squib".

Robin Harris, Marlborough, Wiltshire

A friend who has been one told me that plumbers used to be called "lead bashers".

Bernard Parke, Guildford

In our part of the steel industry, a plumber is known as "leaky".

John Daly, Houston, Renfrewshire

Following recent articles I would suggest that plumbers are also likely to be known as "BA", "MA", "PhD" and so on.

Mr B. Henrym, Birmingham

When I was at university, plumbers were also known as "mechanical engineering undergraduates".

Glenn Haldane, London W12

"Late".

Peter Geoghegan, Formby, Lancashire

Plumbers are generally called "unobtainable" or "very expensive".
Joe McReynolds, Coleraine, Co. Londonderry

A plumber is known as "sir" if you need his services before 2004.
Alun Morris, Cambridge

The word "plumber" is actually used in the same manner as the words "sparky" for electricians and "chippie" for carpenters — that is to say, a tradesman who is a "pipe fitter" is known as a "plumber". The use of the term is now so universal that it has virtually supplanted the original expression.

The origin of the word "plumber", of course, arises from the former use by pipe fitters of lead pipes — the Latin for lead being *plumbum*.
Gordon Perfect, Hemingby, Lincolnshire

In my days in Lima, Peru, the local populace referred to a plumber as a *"gasfitero"*. The derivation from the English is obvious.
Tom Hawthorn, Lowestoft

There have been recent reports about plumbers earning £150,000 p.a. Perhaps a plumber should be known as a "flush"?
Hermione Doyle, Swanley, Kent

The dignity of the few of their number in this area is enhanced by their preference for being known as "privy counsellors".
John Sclanders, Horsted Keynes, West Sussex

In Germany a plumber is known as a *Klempner*, ie, someone who "clamps things". In Spain the word for a plumber is *fontanero* — a man who is perhaps adept at both creating and dealing with "fountains".

Does this tell us anything about the differing psychology of the two nationalities? I think it does. *"Olé! El Fontanero!"* has a much more cheerful ring to it than the workaday *"Hier kommt der Klempner"*.
Paul Adamson, Eskdale Green, Cumbria

What is the longest palindrome that makes sense?

John O'Byrne, Dublin

"Lewd I did live, evil did I dwel" is 24 letters long and has a slightly "Shakespearean" ring to it. Or, "ten animals I slam in a net" and "A man, a plan, a canal, Panama" both have 21.

Malcolm Hutchinson, Darlington

Seen on a blackboard in an Oxford cafe:

"Stressed, no tips, spit on desserts".

This 28-letter palindrome probably had the desired effect.

Sean O'Kelly, Lechlade, Gloucestershire

Two people discussing a cure for warts:

"Straw? No, too stupid a fad. I put soot on warts." (35 letters)

Lesley Byers, Bournemouth

"Are we not drawn onward, we few, drawn onward to new era?" Forty-three letters and it just makes sense, particularly if spoken by George W. Bush.

Nick Mawer, London SE3

In the book *Codebreakers* Jack Good says that Peter Hilton, a colleague at Bletchley, "once spent a sleepless night composing the masterly palindrome":

"Doc note, I dissent. A fast never prevents a fatness. I diet on cod." This has 51 letters.

Professor R. F. Churchhouse, Cardiff

The poet Alastair Reid created this 85-character palindrome: "T Eliot, top bard, notes putrid tang emanating, is sad. I'd assign it a name: 'Gnat-dirt upset on drab pot toilet'."

However, that most ambitious and successful investigator of verbal challenges, Georges Perec (1936–82), compiled a palindrome of more than 5,000 characters in French, which was published in one of the collections of work by members of the Oulipo literary group.

David Fisher, Brighton

Our Cretan waiter in a skiing resort in the Tirol this month told us of a palindrome, which he said is still to be seen inscribed in Santa Sophia in Istanbul. It reads:

"ΝΙΨΟΝ ΑΝΟΜΗΜΑΤΑ ΜΗ ΜΟΝΑΝ ΟΨΙΝ" (25 letters)
The meaning is "Wash your sins (away) and not only your face."
Michael Blair, London SE24

During my youth in Switzerland, I heard the following palindrome: *Eine treue Familie bei Lima feuerte nie.* ("One loyal family near Lima never fired.") The saying was that a German journalist, sent to Peru to cover one of that country's revolutions, came up with this palindrome after getting bored by the relative peace of his quarters.
Hendrik O. Vollers, Bodorgan, Anglesey

There is a 33-letter Latin hexameter about gnats, attributed (no doubt spuriously) to Virgil.
IN GIRUM IMUS NOCTES ET CONSUMIMUR IGNI ("In circles we move by night, and are consumed by the fire").
Raphael Loewe, London N2

The Latin palindrome "*In girum imus noctes et consumimur igni*" is a good idea, but depends on the misspelling of "*gyrum*". And its claim to be a hexameter is dubious, with no caesura in the third or any other foot.
Ian Bently, Shipley, West Yorkshire

In the mid-1920s the headmaster of my preparatory school was a large and slightly eccentric scholar named E. F. "Jumbo" Johns. He gave us one palindrome which he said was the longest. It is the form of a Latin elegiac couplet, and is supposed to have been extemporised by the Devil, whom St Martin (I think it was) had turned into an ass on which he was riding and using his stick on the way to Rome:
   Signa te, signa; temere me tangis et angis.
   Roma tibi subito motibus ibit amor.
   This may be roughly rendered "Sign yourself, sign yourself (with the Cross); it is rash of you to strike and hurt me. You will soon reach your beloved Rome by my motions." The hexameter and pentameter are, of course, separate palindromes, and the Latin is mediaeval.
   It is surely a tribute to Jumbo's teaching that I have remembered this palindrome for nearly 80 years!
B. W. Robinson, London SW10

Depending on the silliness of your sense of humour, you can have some fun with variations of the famous "Able was I ere I saw Elba" palindrome. My favourite is the enigmatic:

"Lana C. Ladaug was I ere I saw Guadalcanal."

Stephen J. Whitaker, Stoke Poges, Buckinghamshire

Even more ingenious than the examples offered by your correspondents is the Minuet and Trio of Haydn's Symphony No 47 in G (1772). The whole movement sounds the same whether played forwards or backwards. The palindrome is note for note perfect in every part — strings, two oboes and two horns. And it is charming music. Few listeners would detect what is going on unless they were studying the score.

Roger Coombs, Goudhurst, Kent

Is it true that the word "hello" was invented only for use with the telephone? What greeting was used previously?

Nick Elsley, London N20

"Hello" is the latest version (late-19th-century) of earlier utterances to attract attention, but it has evolved to a greeting because of the telephone. Middle English had "hallow" (Old French "halloer") "to pursue with shouting", hence "halloo" as a hunting cry to hounds. Variants on this sound are "holla" and "hollo" (16th-century), "hallo" (18th-century) and "hullo" (mid-19th).

"Hello", the latest, was originally to attract the attention of anyone receiving and so ensure that the line was live. It is easy to see how this opening word would become heard as a greeting when its original use had become redundant.

Christopher Nutt, Cambridge

"Hello" (also hallo, hullo, etc) predates the telephone. Dickens used it. In Chapter 11 of *Great Expectations* (1860), Herbert Pocket greets Pip with "Hollo, young fellow!"

Pip comments: "Hollo being a general observation which I have usually observed to be best answered by itself, I said 'Hollo!', politely omitting 'young fellow'."

Peter Hopkins, Loughborough

There is no single English word synonymous with the German word *Schadenfreude*. If we could invent one, what would it be?

Raj Kothari, Bridport, Dorset

"Gloating".

Michael Knight, Geneva

While working in Germany I was asked by a German colleague how "*Schadenfreude*" translates into English. Knowing of no single-word translation, I looked it up and found it translated as "malicious glee".

What is odd is that I found this information not in a dictionary, but in a publication entitled *Helpful Hints and Friendly Advice for the Traveller*.

Paul Arden-Griffith, London SE18

What about the Beowulfian "mischanceglee" or the more Orwellian "woedelight"?

John Mumford, Glasgow

Flopjoy? Fallglee? Tripgiggle? Failfun? Crashlaugh? There are lots.

James McGrory, Tashkent, Uzbekistan

What about "malisfaction"?

M. F. Wilson, Doncaster

"Servesuright".

John O'Byrne, Dublin

A musical one from junior school:
    "La la la-la la".

Alan Mercado, Hornchurch, Essex

"Fiveone".

Peter Mottley, Pangbourne, Berkshire

Why don't parents use personal pronouns to refer to themselves when addressing young children? For example, why do we say "Give it to Daddy" instead of "Give it to me"?

Bryan Gabriel, Horsham, West Sussex

The reason we say "Give it to Daddy" to a young child is our assumption that they are not yet old enough to appreciate that the pronoun "me" does not have a fixed reference, and so may be confused. Dr Noam Chomsky, with his theory of wired in grammatical understanding, might take a different view, of course.

Robert Gooding, Farnham, Surrey

Because if you don't do this, they don't know who you are, and being acute of hearing they address you by your given name just as other people do. My niece Millie, aged two, has only recently begun to use Mummy and Daddy, having until a few weeks ago called her parents Margie and Nicky, and addressed her grandmother (a frequent visitor) as "Mum".

Liz Woods, Godolphin Cross, Cornwall

My parents did not believe in "baby talk". From birth they used my name in an adult way, as a form of address or to attract attention. Otherwise, they spoke to me using normal personal pronouns.

As speech developed, I referred to myself as "you" and to other people as "I" or "me", unless trying to attract a particular individual's attention when I would call for "Mummy" or whoever. By age two, I was a real chatterbox, but difficult to understand. I would express thirst by saying "Do you want a drink?" and indicate a fallen toy saying "You have dropped it". "Have I seen pussy?" would in fact be asking whether the person to whom I was talking knew where the cat was.

In vain my parents tried to unscramble the pronouns, but their explanations merely confused things further, my word usage becoming more unintelligible as my vocabulary increased. When I had just turned four, my mother's illness caused me to be boarded with an uncle in Derby. He did a magnificent job. I returned home to London a few months later grammatically perfect, and with a broad Derbyshire accent still detectable 50 years on.

Joan Horton, Slough, Berkshire

Whatever happened to Esperanto? Does anyone still learn or speak it?

Martin Walters, Princes Risborough, Buckinghamshire

Jes — mi.

Adrian Brodkin, London N2

Esperanto vivas kaj estas sana kaj cilande havas hejmon en Barlaston — or — "Esperanto is alive and well and in this country has a home at Barlaston."

Barlaston, near Stoke-on-Trent, is the new headquarters of the Esperanto Association of Britain, which moved there from London a couple of years ago.

English-speakers, generally, think everybody should speak English, despite it being so imprecise and difficult to learn. So Esperanto — logical, clear, simple — is not so strong in Britain (having 1,000 or so speakers) as in some other parts of the world, particularly Eastern Europe, South America and the Far East.

The annual congress of the Universal Esperanto Association is held in various parts of the world. It is the only international conference that does not require interpreters. Everything is in Esperanto and understood by everybody.

G. D. Hammerton, Secretary of the East Midlands Esperanto
Federation, Derby

Two important things have affected the language in recent years. One is the fall of the Berlin Wall and the collapse of the Soviet Union. This has opened up Eastern Europe, the area where Esperanto was born, to the rest of the world and made a huge difference to international communication and freedom to travel.

The second is the internet. There was a time when communication between Esperantists in different continents was dependent on postal services that could sometimes take weeks and weeks. Now you can e-mail a request in Esperanto and receive replies from all over the world within days. Only the other day I sent a message to an Esperantist in Germany regarding a "twinning" project between our regions, and the next day I received his reply. Readers wishing to know whether anyone still speaks Esperanto should type the word into a search engine and prepare to be astonished by the results.

Elizabeth Stanley, Stroud, Gloucestershire

The answer can be found at the mere click of the mouse. A search for "Esperanto" on any search engine on the internet (Google will bring up 1,230,000 pages), gives access to all the evidence one may need to learn that Esperanto is the living language of a vibrant international community, served by hundreds of journals and daily and weekly radio broadcasts.

Vatican Radio is one of the regular broadcasters, and the Pope uses Esperanto among the many other languages in his Easter blessing "Urbi et Orbi".

Brian O'Sullivan, Sheffield

When we tease somebody, why do we "pull their leg"?
Richard Doubleday, Bath

At the end of the 1980s, my first job after leaving school was as an exhibition guide at Madame Tussaud's. In the Chamber of Horrors they had a real gallows and one of the stories we used to tell the customers about it was the derivation of the term "to pull someone's leg".

Many years before the invention of the "drop" — the trapdoor the criminal fell through to ensure that the noose broke his neck — there was a court case where a relative of a hanged criminal was accused of bribing the executioner to pull the condemned man's legs to quicken his demise. Without the drop, hanging was a lengthy affair with the victim struggling for many minutes while the noose strangled him.

This form of bribery was supposedly quite common but the judge of the case didn't seem to think so. He found it so preposterous and unbelievable that he threw the case out — hence "pulling your leg".
Steve Donoughue, London NW1

Has anyone with a "-son" format surname (e.g. Thompson, Johnson) ever managed to identify the actual person in their family tree whose first name (i.e. Tom, John) gave the family its surname?

Pete Thompson, Bath

My first forebear was Thomas (or Tom), one of the several illegitimate offspring of John of Gaunt, first Duke of Lancaster (1346–99). Like the others, he was acknowledged by his father and appointed to the post of Warden of the Lune Marshes on the ducal estates in northern Lancashire. Family legend has it that he naturally became known as Tom of the Lune, and his son in the custom of the times as Tom of the Lune's son — hence Tomlinson.

Some corroboration of this story was provided by the grant of a coat of arms by Queen Elizabeth I to another of my forebears in the 1590s. Although this was some 200 years later, the story of the family's origin must have been well attested, as the arms are surmounted by a commoner's visor bearing a ducal coronet. By definition, an acknowledged male descendant of a duke (represented by the coronet) could only be a commoner if he was of illegitimate origin.

Not all Tomlinsons are necessarily of the same origin, as there is at least one other derivation for the name. However, I suspect that those with a strong Lancashire connection probably are.

David Tomlinson, London SW9

The wording of Pete Thompson's question suggests that he imagines the practice of changing surnames from generation to generation died out a very long time ago.

This may be so in England, but is not true of the Shetland Isles, from which my paternal family came.

One strand of my family tree is: Olaf Nicolson, whose son was William Olafson, and then successively, Thomas Williamson (who died in 1667), Daniel Thompson, William Danielson and Laurence Williamson. It is only at the next generation that the surname "Williamson" stuck, so we have Gifford Thomas Williamson, whose daughter was Martha Williamson, whose name not only confirms the adoption of a single surname, but also the English language illogicality of a woman called "-son".

Martha Williamson was one of my great-great grandmothers, and probably born about 1810. So William Danielson, whose name has led to the "Williamson" strand in my family tree, was probably born 70 to 90 years before that.

As the older parts of my family tree are sketchy on the female side, I am not sure whether this Shetlandic retention of a Scandinavian naming practice (which still exists, for example, in Iceland) into the 18th century at least, included the more logical practice of using the female suffix "-*dochter*".

Richard Tulloch, Salisbury

My maiden name was Jackson and I know how and why it was adopted.

In 1945 my father — a second-generation Polish immigrant — was due to go to Germany with the British Army and he was told quite categorically that his name had to be changed, as being called Wenglawski would be a danger to his life. He therefore changed his name to Jackson. The reason was that his father's name was Jack and in synagogue services he was used to being called Aleck, son of Jack.

It was a shortlived family line, since he had three daughters but the name lives on as my son's second name.

Michelle Haynes, London NW7

I am sure that the Adamsons must have done so.

Archie Thomson, Whitby, North Yorkshire

What is the origin of the saying regarding the curate's egg being good in parts?

Stephen Hirst, Sheffield

As most people will appreciate, a curate is at the bottom of the priestly pecking order, poorly paid and with little job security.

On November 9, 1895, *Punch* featured a cartoon by George Du Maurier which showed a timid curate having breakfast in his bishop's home. The bishop is saying: "I'm afraid you have got a bad egg, Mr Jones", to which the curate replies, in a desperate attempt not to give offence: "Oh, no, my Lord, I assure you that parts of it are excellent!"

Readers liked this exchange so much that the cartoon led to the catchphrase "good in parts". The phrase "curate's egg" itself means something that is partly good and partly bad and so not wholly satisfactory.

Christopher Hirsh, Walton-on-Thames, Surrey

The humour lies in the dilemma of the curate, who can neither deny the truth of the bishop's statement, nor agree with it, since to do so would cast doubt on the hospitality of his host and patron. He therefore hits on this brilliant compromise and face-saving reply, which is of course nonsense, since an egg is either good or bad — it can't be partly good.

Further spice is added by the way the curate is drawn as a stringy poor fellow. In contrast, the bishop is portly, clearly no stranger to good living.

Paul Smith, Matlock, Derbyshire

Your correspondent maintains that "a curate is at the bottom of the priestly pecking order". Actually he or she is not. As vicar of Exning with the Chapel of Landwade in Suffolk, I am the curate of the parish, as I have been assigned the "cure of souls". The person that assists me in this is the assistant curate and she is the one with little job security.

As to the issue of being "poorly paid", perhaps I had better not comment.

Canon Simon Pettitt, Newmarket, Suffolk

How does the word "drag" come to mean the attire adopted by men to give them the appearance of being women?

E. Skwierczynska, Oxford

"Drag" in this sense seems to derive from theatrical slang in the 1860s and 1870s for male stage actors in England who were required to play the roles of women (or of men obliged to disguise themselves as women). This may explain why the expression is still mostly used of actors and stage personalities rather than merely of cross-dressers. It is thought that the meaning came about because of the hindrance (or "drag") of women's apparel, especially skirts, on supposedly more active masculine movements.

On the other hand, since 150 years earlier, the word as a hunting term has also borne the meaning of a type of lure involving scent – which may have influenced some Victorian people's understanding, if not, perhaps, some modern people's.

Mike Darton, Preston St Mary, Suffolk

The association of cross-dressing and sexual relations between men had become proverbial by the mid 18th century, notably with the revelations of London's "molly houses" (male brothels). To go "on the drag" or "flash the drag" was to wear female attire to solicit men. Transvestites and transvestite performers were said to be "in drag", a term from thieves' cant that compared the train of a gown to the drag or brake on a coach. It entered theatrical parlance from homosexual slang around 1870.

Not every cross-dressing performer likes the term "drag". The late Rex Jameson, who was better known in female attire as the Cockney charlady Mrs Shufflewick, always referred to himself as "a comedian in women's clothing".

Patrick Newley, London SW16

Did North American Indians really greet each other by saying "How!"? If so, was it common to all Indian tribes, and what exactly did it mean?

John Gannon, Cambridge

"How" is the English transliteration of the Siouan word *hau* or *hao*, meaning "good", and is part of the greeting *hau kola* which meant "all is well, comrade" and "remain well, comrade". This could be used between comparative (male) strangers and esoteric mutual sociability among (male) members of a council or sweat-lodge. The gesture of a raised hand with open palm was initially a quite separate token of peaceful intentions between comparative strangers but became associated with the verbal greeting through frequency of usage in confrontation with white men wielding guns.

Tribes that spoke in such terms were or are the Dakota/Lakota/ Nakota-speaking peoples of the Sioux nation in the western and north-western United States.

Mike Darton, Preston St Mary, Suffolk

Surely "How!" is an abbreviation of the northern English greeting "How do?" which in turn is an abbreviation of the more formal "How do you do?"

Tim Spanton, London El

The Rev William Spooner is best remembered for transposing letters at the beginning of words, eg, "You have hissed my mystery lectures" and " You have tasted a whole worm". How many authentic spoonerisms are there?

John O'Byrne, Dublin

According to William Hayter's 1977 biography of William Spooner, the answer is not many. Most were made up by undergraduate wits or W. W. Merry, the Rector of Lincoln College. It has been authenticated that he called "Dr Childe's friend" "Dr Friend's child"; that he referred to the story of the Flood as "barrowed from Bobylon" and when officiating at a wedding he spoke of the husband and wife "loifully jawned in holy matrimony".

Spooner himself admitted to giving out the hymn in chapel as "Kinquering Kongs" but doubt was thrown on even this by his wife, who pointed out that the titles of hymns were never given out — they were on the printed sheets.

One authentic "physical spoonerism" is recorded. At a dinner party Spooner upset a salt cellar on the tablecloth, and reaching for the claret decanter, poured claret on the salt till he had produced a little purple mound.

Hugh Symons, Kingston upon Thames, Surrey

Mr Spooner always denied saying any of "those things". He is, however, alleged to have had the following exchange with a fellow of his college on meeting him in the quad: "Do dine in tonight and meet our new fellow, Stanley Casson."

"I am Stanley Casson."
"Never mind, come anyway."

David Jones, Cambridge

I do not know how authentic this is, but he is said to have once referred to Queen Victoria as "our queer old dean".

E. Housley, Edinburgh

My favourite, and I believe authenticated, example of a transposition is Dr Spooner seeing his wife onto a train at Oxford station. Shortly before the train departed, he kissed the porter and gave his wife sixpence.

Richard Tarran, Abergavenny, Monmouthshire

My old friend, the late Sir Christopher Cox, knew "the Spoo" and could mimic his slow and precise accent.

Christopher, the source of many of William Hayter's stories in his 1977 biography, vouched for none of the famous swapped initial letters (he sometimes allowed the toast "Our queer old Dean"), but had many instances of the transposition of ideas.

For instance, he once pointed out to Christopher an old lady in Oxford dressed all in black: "Poor dear, her late husband. So sad. Eaten by missionaries".

Patrick Martin, Winchester, Hampshire

What was the original white elephant that cost so much and was of so little use?

Andrew McKay, Bradford, West Yorkshire

In ancient Siam, now Thailand, elephants with a very pale or white hide were highly valued and revered, so much so that their owners were required to pamper them. By tradition, if a courtier offended or upset the King the courtier would be given a white elephant. Such a gift was a harsh punishment since the recipient was forced to pay for its upkeep, feed and housing but could not force it to work. He dare not further offend the King by harming the beast or giving it away.

Jack Russell, Hampton, Middlesex

Although I cannot supply a definitive answer, I wonder why my attention was strangely drawn to the photograph of Emile Heskey about six inches to the right of the original question.

Ian Greaves, Sutton Coldfield, Warwickshire

President Bush's speeches seem to consist of short sentences separated by long pauses. Is there a name for this method of delivery?

Derek Martin, Marlow, Buckinghamshire

The President has been taught a style that goes back to Greek times. I would call it an oratory style.

There are two sorts of pause. First, the pause before speaking. It raises expectation and gives the impression that the matter is being given due thought. Hitler excelled with a 30-second pause before launching into his speech. That pause is also a useful device to those who wish to read from a script verbatim, as it makes it appear that the idea had just been thought through.

The second pause has a different effect. By pausing after a short phrase (often not a sentence) the words hang in the air and can be digested by the audience. Churchill understood this perfectly. The pause also had another effect when accompanied by steady eye contact. The speaker gives the impression of seeking a response from the audience. Most people at the end of an idea start to look away as they generate something new. The style can be extremely effective but also can become stilted and overdone. The trick is to use other more fluid bursts to provide a contrast. Former President Bill Clinton is, I believe, the most adept politician today at using these techniques.

Alastair Grant, London SW14

When did the term "political correctness" first come into common parlance and who first coined it?

L. Pastrone, Windsor

According to Volume 3 (published in 1997) of *Later Additions to the Oxford English Dictionary Second Edition*, the expression "political correctness" appeared first in the American *Political Science Review* in 1948. It is said to have later appeared in *The Washington Post* in 1979; in *The Los Angeles Times* in 1986 and in *The Times* on July 4, 1991 (although, in truth, it actually first appeared in *The Times* on July 10, 1986).

Christopher Simpson, Leicester

Social philosophers in American universities during the 1990s are responsible for the spread of this scourge of new morality which has lead to much irritation to ordinary people, who normally try to utilise "common sense" in their everyday language.

In trying to avoid offending, denigrating or insulting minorities who may be perceived to be disadvantaged in some way, such as by physical disability, race, gender, class, religious or political leanings, PC words replace those in common usage leading to quite extreme ludicrous definitions, which actually often draw attention to the particular perceived disadvantage, and label a user as racist, sexist, ageist or just biased. "Tall", "fat", "thin", "black", "old", "crippled" and even "Christmas" are examples of words which now have to be used with care, otherwise the wrath of the self-appointed accusers will fall on the users. Big Brother has arrived together with Newspeak.

A. R. Stopford, Leicester

What does "bang out of order" actually mean?
David Wright, Derby

When something goes "bang" it invariably then goes "out of order".
Clive Hampson, Stockport, Cheshire

"Bang" meaning "completely" is given by the *OED* as of 19th-century origin. "Out of order", meaning (of behaviour or of a person) "improper, in the wrong, antisocial, not conforming with accepted norms", is an old London expression. "Order" here means either "regular procedure or rule" (as in Parliament) or as in "natural order" (of a moral or social system).

Lawyers used to joke of the East End of London that the local people acknowledged only two offences in their common law: the minor one of "being out of order" and the aggravated one of "being well out of order", the latter meriting complete social ostracism.
Christopher Nutt, Cambridge

When a new word enters a language which has gender-specific nouns, how is the gender determined?
Mark James, Birmingham

Greek uses male, female and neuter. Most new words in the language are English, and I was told by my Greek language teacher that all foreign words — "sex", "striptease", "rally", "cinema", "nightclub" — are prefixed neuter.

Ruth Standring, Athens

It would seem that, in French, most Anglo-Americanisms are masculine: *le hot-dog, le weekend, le hamburger, le match, le foot, le rugby, le score, le scotch* (sticky-tape). Two feminine ones, however, spring to mind: *la garden-party* and *la star*.

In the world of information technology, the word for IT itself is *l'informatique*, which is feminine, but very many of the words to do with IT are masculine: *l'ordinateur, le logiciel, le matériel, un e-mail, le traitement de texte, le disque sauvegarde, le bogue* and *le téléchargement*.

In modern medicine, many words are masculine, eg, *le SIDA, le triple pontage*; and in modern sporting activities, eg, *le parapente, le surf*. Maybe in 100 years' time all French nouns will be masculine, and we shall find the language much easier to learn.

Diana Lloyd, Malmesbury, Wiltshire

I put this question to a French friend. He looked puzzled, and said: "Nobody *decides* the gender of a new noun. You just know instinctively. For example, *télévision* is feminine because *vision* is feminine. And *la BBC* is feminine because it is *une société*."

"What about *le téléviseur* or *le téléphone*?" I asked. "Well, they're objects," he replied. "So is *la table*, yet that's feminine," I countered. At that point, he did what all French people do in such a situation. "*Mais, c'est comme ça*," he shrugged.

Ralph Watmough, Saint-Cosme-en-Vairais, France

What exactly is a "square meal" and why is it served on round plates?

Kevin Cullen, Derby

The term "square meal" is one of the many phrases in use today that can trace its origins to the Royal Navy of at least the 18th century. On board HMS *Victory*, for example, Nelson's surviving flagship, sailors ate their meals from square wooden plates. As life ashore 200 years ago was pretty tough for most people, by joining the Royal Navy you at least had the advantage of eating "three square meals" a day, although they were mostly grim fare.

Ian Pollard, Gosport, Hampshire

The edges of sailors' square plates had a raised section called a "fiddle". If you distracted your neighbour's attention, you could scoop food over the fiddle on to your own plate, thus giving rise to the expression of "being on the fiddle". There is a square plate in the museum of the Chatham Naval Dockyard.

Charles Oliver, Gravesend, Kent

In the Middle Ages, only the affluent ate off plates; their meals were fuller and more substantial than those eaten by the lower orders. Their wooden plates were, however, square or rectangular and often called trenchers; hence the origin of the phrase, "a good trencherman". The plates were square or rectangular rather than round because it was easier to shape them this way from a log using an axe.

John Clegg, Hoylake, Cheshire

3. KNOW YOUR HISTORY

When did the Romans stop speaking Latin and start speaking Italian?

David Phillips, Margate, Kent

A spoken version of Latin different from classical Latin existed even under the Roman republic. In the later Roman Empire the popular language diverged more and more from the Latin taught in schools. This vulgar Latin developed features which later became characteristic of the Romance languages, for example the formation of the perfect tense with the past participle (*habeo acceptam*, similar to the modern Italian *ho accettato*) in place of literary Latin's simple perfect. With the disintegration of the western Roman Empire, literary Latin continued to be the only language taught in schools, while various local vernaculars increasingly diverged from the literary language and from each other.

The earliest written records of local vernaculars in Italy date from the 9th century. Formal Latin continued to be the only spoken language of instruction in Italian schools until about 1200, even though by then the local vernaculars, more similar to the modern language than to Latin, seem to have prevailed as the spoken language of everyday life. Latin remained the dominant spoken language of schools and universities in Italy well into the 16th century.

Robert Black, University of Leeds

I have heard that the nursery rhyme about the Grand Old Duke of York and his 10,000 men is a satire on a real person. If so, who was he?

Bernard Beard, Bowdon, Cheshire

I believe that this nursery rhyme refers to an incident in the Flanders campaign of 1794 against the French forces, when the second son of George III, Frederick, the Duke of York and Albany, while manoeuvring troops for a more advantageous tactical placement, did indeed "march them up to the top of a hill, then march them down again". One can imagine the troops of the time, in common with troops of any period, being less than enamoured of this seemingly pointless effort.

His lack of aptitude in field operations did not harm his later career in the War Office and Horse Guards, where he was instrumental in pushing through a number of much needed reforms regarding military administration and procurement.

Corporal Robert Knight, Aldershot, Hampshire

Your correspondent has produced an ingenious theory. How sad it is to spoil a good story by inconvenient facts. Frederick, Duke of York and Albany, (1763–1827) was never Colonel or Colonel-in-Chief of the 3rd Dragoons. He was Commander in Chief of the British Army from 1798 to 1809 and from 1811 to his death, when the 3rd King's Own Dragoons formed but one regiment in the Army. The document describing elaborate dress, referred to by Bolitho, was dated 1751, twelve years before the Duke of York was born.

I have always understood that the nursery rhyme originated from the Duke of York's lack of decision when commanding the expedition to Helder in 1799. It would seem certain that it had no connection with the 3rd King's Own Dragoons.

Colonel A. H. N. Reade, Wallingford, Oxfordshire

Corporal Knight's explanation of the nursery rhyme may well be right, but I lived for 28 years in Belgium and can state that I have never seen a hill in Flanders, though there may be one or two small ones tucked away well off the beaten track, though hardly large enough to accommodate 10,000 men marching up and down. There is a sort of hillock at Waterloo, but this was built artificially after the battle there, long after the time of George III, and Waterloo is not in Flanders anyway.

Richard Dunn, Cambridge

I was taught at school that the reason for the rhyme was that his men were shipped separately from their equipment. The arrival of the latter was delayed so that marching was the only soldiering the men could do in the meantime.

His Honour Judge Peter Heppel QC, Hull Combined Court Centre

According to Lyn Macdonald, in her book *1914*, the nursery rhyme referred to the town of Cassel, which lay on the summit of a steep hill on the coastal plain of Flanders. The main road to the coast climbed up to the summit and down again to the foot of the hill on the other side. The reason for the road running this way, rather than simply sticking to the flat plain, went back to the days when Cassel was a fortress. Once the Grand Old Duke of York had got to the top of the hill, he had no choice but to march his men down again because that was the only route available.

John Yarnall, Kingston upon Thames

The origin of the nursery rhyme was carefully investigated by the late Colonel Alfred Burne in his biography of Frederick the Duke of York and Albany, *The Noble Duke of York* (1949). He stated: "As for the hill, Mount Cassell in Belgium is sometimes pointed to as the spot, but there can be no substance in this; the nearest the Duke ever got to Mount Cassell was over ten miles away. Nor is there any event in his military career that remotely resembles the operation described in the jingle. Most of the country over which he operated, whether in the Flanders or Helder campaigns, is, as everyone knows, flat; there are no hills worthy of the name. Nor did the Duke take his army forward and then reverse the process, whether up a hill or not." Burne concluded that the jingle may have originated from an old nursery rhyme, dating back at least to 1594, which ran:

The King of France went up the hill

With twenty thousand men;

The King of France came down the hill

And never went up again.

Burne continues that "some nimble-witted detractor of the Duke unscrupulously adapted the old rhyme to the new subject." He also believed that the Duke, contrary to received opinion, was as competent a military commander as he was later a reforming administrator.

Gladwyn Turbutt, London W11

The Duke of York, second son of George III, was certainly the Commander-in-Chief of the 3rd or King's Own Regiment of Dragoons. The reason for the nursery rhyme was probably just jealousy and mockery. In *The Galloping Third*, Hector Bolitho describes the regiment's elegant uniforms, splendid horses, and pay more than twice that of foot soldiers. Yet from their records he finds that they were but remotely concerned with England's wars, in Europe, India and North America. The main part of the regiment spent the long years moving about England and Scotland, to the north, to the south, to east and to west, employed in harmless duties, putting down riots, chasing smugglers, helping out in the great floods near Peterborough in 1795 when the south bank of the River Nene gave way. Even Parliament became critical because so many soldiers tramped about Britain and never went to war.

Such grand uniforms did not mean that the private soldier was yet received with widespread admiration, says Bolitho. The majority of men, when they left the Army, had a "bleak outlook", and lived in "little better than professional beggary". What better reason could there be for the ridicule suggested by the nursery rhyme?

Beryl Smedley, Ferring, West Sussex

Why does the tax year start each year on April 6?

Kiran Patel, Reigate, Surrey [20/03/02]

Accounts were traditionally payable in Britain on one of the four "Quarter Days" — on the 25th of March, June, September and December, while the tax year itself ended on Lady Day, March 25. When, in Britain, the Gregorian calendar was introduced in 1752, the bypassing of the 11 "stolen" days meant that March 25 became April 5, and the tax year therefore began on April 6.

The choice of Lady Day for the tax year reflected the fact that, under the Julian calendar, the actual year in Britain had begun since the 14th century on March 25 (and before that on 25 December). The adoption of the Gregorian calendar thus also established January 1 as New Year's Day.

Malcolm Oliver, East Linton, East Lothian

During the changeover in 1752, Parliament took pains to legislate details of the changeover to minimise problems with banking, contracts, birthdays, holidays and sundry private and public issues. For instance, no rents, interest or wages would be paid for the 11 lost days. Many people did not accept the loss, and protests and riots occurred. Even the bankers of the City of London rebelled against the confusion: they refused to pay taxes on the usual date of March 25, 1753. They paid up 11 days later on April 5, which was then adopted as the end of the tax year.

Phil Moore, Brentwood, Essex

While Malcolm Oliver is correct in referring to the traditional Quarter Days, they are not the 25th of each month. They are:

Lady Day — March 25

St John's Day — June 24

Michaelmas — September 29

Christmas Day — December 25

Easily remembered as apart from Christmas Day, the number of letters in the month is the 20-somethingth day. (March 25, June 24, etc)

Tony Watson, Twyford, Berkshire

The responses to this question printed so far have missed one crucial piece of information. My understanding is that, notwithstanding settlement of rental and other dues on Lady Day, the fiscal year prior to 1752 ended on March 24.

Following the date change, the fiscal year was extended by not only 11 days for those lost in September 1752, but also a further day for the loss of February 29, 1753, which under the outgoing Julian calendar would have been a leap day.

Income tax, of course, was not introduced by Pitt until 1799.

C. E. Bumpsteed, Sutton Coldfield, West Midlands

When were the First and Second Reichs in existence?

Malcolm B. Harris, London NW2

The First Reich dated from 962, and the reign of Otto I, the Great, Saxon king and emperor, until 1806 and Napoleon's "Confederation of the Rhine". The Second Reich began in 1871 with German unification and Wilhelm I, with Frederick III reigning 99 days in 1888, and finally ended with Wilhelm II abdicating in 1918.

The term "Third Reich" was coined in 1923 by Moeller van den Bruck, a German writer, to describe a future ideal German state, and adopted by the Nazis who did not acknowledge its source.

Michael Austin, Brighton

When slaves were taken to America they must have taken with them their native African languages. Do any recognisable remnants of these languages exist in North America today?

Terry Ansell, Rickmansworth, Hertfordshire

If you consider North America to start at the Panama Canal and therefore to include countries such as Belize, Honduras and Nicaragua, then recognisable remnants of African languages definitely do exist. Last year, while helping to train Garifuna beekeepers on the Honduran Caribbean coast, I was amazed to discover that I understood some words in their language.

Although the training was conducted in Spanish, the principal language of Honduras, the Garifuna have their own language which has Bantu and Carib origins. My second language is Swahili, which evolved from Bantu and Arabic (even though Swahili originated on the east coast of Africa, not the west from whence the Garifuna were probably shipped).

The Garifuna are reported to be the survivors of two ships which were shipwrecked in the Caribbean Windward Islands (off St Vincent) while on their way to becoming slaves in the West Indies. Those who survived married the local lighter skinned Carib women but retained much of their own language and culture. They were never fully enslaved and after backing the French against the British in St Vincent on a number of occasions, they were finally deported to Roatan in the now Honduran Bay Islands (some going directly to the mainland when a ship was captured by the Spanish).

After much hardship the survivors spread far afield in search of work. As well as on the Atlantic Coast of Central America, Garifuna communities are now reportedly found in North America as far afield as New York, New Orleans and Los Angeles. While their distinctive Punta music is quite well known in other parts of the world, their native Garifuna language is not.

John Goodman, Aberdour, Fife

If the Northern Irish ever vote to leave the United Kingdom, will it be necessary to take the St Patrick's Cross off the Union Flag? Will this also change the Commonwealth countries' flags which contain the Union Flag?

Ron Wigley, Sutton Coldfield, Warwickshire

A red saltire was included in the Union Flag in 1801 to mark the Act of Union with Ireland. However, there is no historical link between the red saltire and St Patrick, nor was it linked to territory in Ireland. The red saltire used in Ireland most likely derives from the emblem of the

Dukes of Burgundy, which was a ragged St Andrew's saltire cross. This emblem became common across the Habsburg inheritance of Burgundy, Spain and Austria, and by the time of the Battle of Pavia in 1525 it had been simplified to a red plain saltire. This red saltire was incorporated in various battle flags during the 16th century and was commonly associated with Catholic and Spanish factions. It is likely that the emblem was carried to Ireland by the continental mercenary troops imported by the Earl of Tyrone in the 1570s, though it may also be linked to flags of Irish emigré mercenaries serving in Catholic armies in European wars. It is known that the Spanish regiments of Ultonia and Hibernia still had a core of Irish soldiers at the beginning of the 19th century, and that the regimental flags contained the original Burgundian ragged red St Andrew's saltire.

As the red saltire is thus not particularly connected with territory in Ireland, there is no reason why it should be dropped from the Union Flag should Northern Ireland leave the UK. The form of Commonwealth countries' flags is a matter for them to determine. However, the Union Flag does also appear on a non Commonwealth flag. The state flag of Hawaii contains the Union Flag, commemorating the European "discovery" of the islands. Noticeably, Hawaii uses the modern version of the Union Flag, not the version that would have been used in Captain Cook's day.

Russell Vallance, Royal Artillery Museum, Woolwich, London SE18

Your correspondent is mistaken about the origins of the saltire ruges, wrongly called "St Patrick's Cross", and its territorial connection with Ireland.

This flag was borne by Maurice FitzGerald as he led the first swath of Cambro-Normans in their invasion of Ireland in 1169. From his children were descended the two great Irish families of the Kildares and the Desmonds who, until their hegemony was crushed, first by Henry VIII and secondly by Elizabeth I, were vast landowners in, and virtual rulers of, Ireland. The saltire is still vested in the arms of their descendants.

Major John FitzGerald, York

In such an event, St Patrick's Cross could remain to represent the land of his birth — Wales — currently not represented in the Union Flag.

Trefor ap Hywel, Betws Diserth, Powys

**When their Central and South American territories obtained
independence, why did the Spanish empire divide into a plethora
of independent states, whereas the end of the Portuguese empire
resulted in just one superstate — Brazil?**
Stephen Browness, Peterborough

When Napoleon invaded the Iberian Peninsula in 1808, the Spanish
Royal Family went into exile in Europe, leaving its American empire
leaderless. Different regions fell under the control of various warlords
and eventually became independent states.

At the same time, the Portuguese Royal Family fled to Brazil, under
British naval protection, and set up court in Rio de Janeiro, where it
continued to govern, so avoiding fragmentation of the country.
Neil B. Thomas, Stafford

The independence, and establishment by 1826 of the Spanish-speak-
ing republics in South America resulted from the political divisions of
the Spanish Empire on the eve of the various revolutions.

The United Mexican States of Central America corresponded to
the Viceroyalty of New Spain. Gran Colombia coincided with the Viceroyalty of New Granada. Peru and Chile formed the Viceroyalty of
Peru and the federation of Argentina, Bolivia and Paraguay once
composed the Viceroyalty of Rio de la Plata.

After their establishment, the year 1828 saw Uruguay declare
independence, following its annexation by the Argentine
Confederation and later Brazil. In 1830 Gran Colombia broke up into
Colombia, Venezuela and Ecuador. Various "liberators" emerged in the
vice-royalties to stamp their authority where possible and form new
republics.

The situation in Brazil was entirely different. Portugal was invaded
by French and Spanish troops in 1807 and the Government, the Prince
Regent appointed by the King and members of the Royal Family fled
to Rio, where they set up the Government of Portugal.

This inversion turned Brazil into a kingdom until it became an
independent empire in 1822, continuing as a monarchy until 1889. In
any event, the population of Brazil was almost all strung along the
Atlantic coast. The interior of the country was largely unexplored.
John Rainsford, Chichester, West Sussex

Why did so many Italian families in the ice-cream trade choose to emigrate to Scotland rather than other parts of the UK?

Christine Greer, Macclesfield, Cheshire [28/06/02]

The Italians first came to Scotland in the late 19th century as peddlers selling plaster saints door-to-door to devout Irish Roman Catholic working-class families in and around Glasgow and Edinburgh. These itinerant traders came mainly from Tuscany and Emilia, from towns and villages around major centres such as Parma, Piacenza, Lucca and Pisa, where there has long been a tradition of craftsmanship in the plastic arts.

They soon realised that there was a more durable market in the shape of a catering service for a largely undernourished industrial working class. Scotland was rich in both fish and potatoes so the Italians went into the fish and chip trade. By 1900 they were prospering and bringing over relatives suffering dire poverty in the motherland. Business expanded with the introduction of mosaic and marble ice-cream parlours and tea rooms where young couples of modest incomes could have a taste of luxury. This attracted immigrants from other parts of Italy, mainly from the south around Cassino and Naples who had traditionally gone to America. Scotland was nearer and the opportunities were just as good. More came after the United States closed the door to further Italian immigrants.

In the meanwhile the Italians spread out all over Scotland. Some retired back to their native villages in Italy, where even today they startle British tourists by suddenly switching from a melodious Italian into English with a broad Glasgow accent.

Peter Muccini, Surbiton, Surrey [04/07/02]

In the early years of the 20th century, large numbers of Italians also came to the South Wales valleys, initially to work in the mines but subsequently becoming purveyors of ice cream and fish and chips, and later the owners of very user-friendly cafes (all of which sold ice cream).

The majority came from the vicinity of Bardi in northern Italy and it seems that the early arrival triggered off an influx of friends and relations. Among the first to set up a cafe was a Bracchi, hence the generic name "Bracchi shops" was applied to all Italian cafes.

In the 1920s the following families could be found in Aberdare alone:

Ferrari, Mascherpa, Rossi, Divito, Servini, Bracchi, Sidoli, Fulgoni, Cardinali, Cruci, Polledri and Tidaldi.

Tom Evans, Aberdare, Glamorgan [04/07/02]

Is there any recorded instance of a duel being fought between two women?

Cindy Thomas, Cranford, Middlesex [29/08/02]

There are several records of duels fought between women, principally in France. In 1828, near Strasbourg, two ladies competing for the love of a painter fought a duel with pistols, and were attended by lady "seconds". Shots were exchanged at 25 paces, but without effect, and the seconds intervened to prevent further shooting. In London in 1790, two ladies of fashion arranged a duel over a similar romantic dispute, and were on the point of firing when they were restrained by a constable who had been sent for by one of the ladies' maids.

On two occasions, in 1827 and 1828, French women fought duels with men. The first, with swords, resulted in severe injuries to the man, while the other, with pistols, was bloodless because the seconds had agreed to load the weapons with powder but no balls.

A Victorian commentator on duelling remarked that women do not fight as often as men, "because of the greater certainty of avenging their injuries by intrigue and slander, whose edge is sharper than the sword".

Colin McKelvie, Culbokie, Ross-shire [05/09/02]

Female duelling, or more strictly, ritual combat, was a traditional feature of upper-class Viking funerals. The dead warrior's wives would fight each other according to traditional rules developed during the first kingdom, for the honour of accompanying their husband on his flaming voyage to Valhalla.

John Clegg, Hoylake, Cheshire [05/09/02]

My grandfather often told of a duel in Cumberland near the River Esk, under the shadow of Silverybield. The ladies in question, Alice Cummings and Martha Lathing, argued (*circa* 1826) over entitlement to land bequeathed to them. One felt she should, through blood, inherit all; the other through her unswerving loyalty, particularly in his latter years, to the testator, one William Chalesworth.

Pistols were used. Both ladies survived, scathed or unscathed.
John Hall, Prenton, Cheshire

I am currently writing a dramatised documentary for television called *The Duelling Story*. Towards the end of the 18th century in England, a Mrs Elphinstone faced her rival Mrs Braddock on the field of honour with swords, and then pistols. The former had questioned her rival's age in public. The affair ended when Mrs Braddock had her wig blown off by Mrs Elphinstone's pistol.

In the 19th century in Austria, a Princess Metternich fought a sword duel with the Countess Kilmannseg after an argument over floral arrangements at a Viennese ball. Both women were wounded. These ladies fought stripped to the waist to prevent clothing being driven into their wounds which was a common cause of infection in those times.

Mark Shelley, Rathnew, Co Wicklow

Countries such as France, Norway and Belgium were occupied by Fascist forces during the Second World War. What was the status of smaller countries such as Andorra, Liechtenstein and San Marino at the time? Were they occupied or did they remain independent?

Chiam Ter Ping, Cardiff

Liechtenstein, though nominally independent, was associated with Austria until 1918 but thereafter linked up with Switzerland. Although it is not officially a Swiss canton, Liechtenstein's frontier with Austria is controlled by Swiss customs and border police. Liechtenstein effectively shared Switzerland's neutrality during the Second World War.

Andorra is technically a "pareage" whereby sovereignty is shared between Spain and France. Since 1607 Andorra has officially been ruled by the Spanish Bishop of Urgel and the French head of state. When France fell in 1940, the Pyrenees frontier was occupied by the German Army. However, occupation of Andorra would have been regarded as a violation of Spanish sovereignty and since Fascist Spain was sympathetic to the Nazis, it would have been an odd act for the Germans. The status of Monaco, on the other hand, was defined by the Treaty of Versailles in 1919 as a territory aligned with France. When

Italy invaded France in 1940, therefore, Monaco was simply treated as part of France and occupied.

San Marino's relationship with Italy was defined by treaty in 1862. The Italian Fascists never occupied San Marino, but San Marino volunteers served with Mussolini's forces. However, the German Army had no scruples about San Marino's sovereignty and Mount Titano in the Republic became a German observation post during the Apennines fighting in 1944.

Russell Vallance, London SE18

I had the good fortune to be a member of the first Ramblers' Association holiday in Andorra after the Second World War (in August 1950), and we had many chats with our sociable hotelier about the wartime days. Andorra appears to have maintained a precarious independence during the war years, but my diary records: "Prisoners used to try to escape through here from France, and the Germans sent police cars into the country after them; the Andorran Army, which then consisted only of six men (it now has 12), had to let them through."

Our hotelier was a Republican refugee from Barcelona, who got out only just ahead of Franco's Army in 1939 and gained sanctuary in Andorra.

Derek J. Way, Heswall, Cheshire

We all know the origin of years, months and days, but whence the week for those not guided by Creation? Do other cultures have a similar period and if so, how long is it and is it based on the concept of a day of rest?

Jon Blok, Banbury, Oxfordshire

At least one aetiology of the week is that it goes back to the lunar calendar used by Sumerian and then Babylonian civilisations. The time taken by the Moon to complete an orbit round the Earth is between 29 and 30 days. The start of a new month was determined by observation. A festival was held at the new moon (Day 1), at half moon (Day 14 or 15) and at first and second quarter (Day 7/8 and 21/22). These approximate to seven-day intervals. However, this explanation does not have to be exclusively Mesopotamian, for many other (if not all) early cultures used lunar calendars.

Dr John MacGinnis, Cambridge

Several years ago my wife and I lived in the town of Canchungo in Guinea Bissau, West Africa. The business calendar, inherited from the former Portuguese colonists, naturally followed a seven-day week, with a market day on Fridays. However, the local Manjaco people held to a five-day week, again with a market held once within the cycle.

When the "traditional" and "European" market days coincided, as they did every 35 days, a "big market" was held, attended by buyers and sellers of livestock from a large area. Why the Manjaco people have a five-day week, I sadly do not know.

Andrew Kleissner, London W12

The development of calendars began in river valleys. The estuarial parts of the Tigris, Euphrates, Indus and Yangtze rivers are all tidal. Tides decrease in height and strength from new moon to the moon's first quarter and increase from the quarter until full moon; this decrease followed by increase in the tides is repeated from full through the third quarter back round to the next new moon.

The tides therefore mark out four parts of a month, each roughly a week long. Crucially, when the sky remains overcast, simple observations of tidal activity enables anyone to know when the moon has changed.

Captain Paul Hughes, Airmyn, Yorkshire

Until 1956, we had only 1st and 3rd class travel on the railways. Prior to that date, was there ever 2nd class? If there was, when and why was it dropped?

Cliff Skudder, Letchworth, Hertfordshire

In the early days of railways there were, in fact, only two classes: first and second. Companies such as the Liverpool and Manchester actually ran separate first and second class trains.

The universal 3rd class was a result of Gladstone's Regulation of the Railways Act of 1844, which required companies to run at least one train in each direction on every route per day, carrying 3rd class passengers in closed carriages, at a fare of no more than 1d per mile (the so-called "parliamentary" trains). Companies often frustrated the intentions of the Act by running these trains at the most inconvenient times possible.

It was the Midland Railway which, in an attempt to steal a march on its rivals, abolished 2nd class on January 1, 1875. In fact, it scrapped 3rd class coaches and rebranded 2nd class vehicles to third, so that 3rd class passengers on the Midland could now travel with 2nd class comfort. Most, but not all, companies eventually followed suit, although 3rd class travel on some remained truly penitential.

However, the LNER retained second class for its London suburban services until 1938, and the Southern on some continental boat trains until after the Second World War.

As your correspondent states, the situation was rationalised in 1956, when 3rd class was renamed 2nd class. It became "standard class" in 1987.

Nicholas Daunt, Up Holland, Lancashire

As a schoolboy in 1937 and 1938, I travelled unescorted daily from Hadley Wood to New Barnet on LNER by 2nd class.

During the war, 2nd class became regarded as an anachronism and the existing 2nd class compartments were regraded as 3rd class. In 1956 the charade was abandoned and the then 3rd class was regraded 2nd, but with no corresponding increase in comfort.

Peter Crawford, Thorpe Mandeville, Northamptonshire

I well remember travelling in a 2nd class railway coach in September 1918. It was my first term at my preparatory school, evacuated from Westgate-on-Sea to North Coker House, near Yeovil.

Lord Brightman, London SW7

My late father, growing up in Germany before the Second World War, recalls that some trains there had a fourth class: windowless cattle-trucks with a narrow ledge around the side upon which more fortunate passengers could rest their posteriors.

Andrew Kleissner, London W12

What happened to Pontius Pilate after the crucifixion of Christ?
John O'Byrne, Dublin

Apart from the reference to Pilate in the gospels of the New Testament, and a rather more detailed account of his dealings as procurator of Judaea recorded by the 1st-century AD Romano-Jewish historian Flavius Josephus, little factual information is known of Pilate before

AD26, when he was appointed Governor, or after the year AD36, when he was recalled to Rome in disgrace.

Sent by Tiberius to rule the notoriously difficult province of Judaea, Pilate seemingly set out deliberately to offend the Jews at every opportunity. For example, he put Roman religious emblems on the coins he minted and set up images of Caesar in the Temple in Jerusalem. These latter he was forced to remove. An inscribed stone discovered in the Roman theatre at Caesarea in 1961 was dedicated to Tiberius by Pilate, who is described as Praefectus ("prefect") and not Procurator. Apart from the apocryphal "Letter of Pontius Pilate" and the "Acts of Pontius Pilate" no letters or other inscriptions by him or to him have been found.

In AD36 Pilate was summoned to Rome by Tiberius on a charge of incompetence, but that Emperor died before his return. According to Eusebius, Pilate was forced to commit suicide by Caligula, while other legends say that he was banished to Vienne in Gaul, where he died.

The Greek Orthodox and Ethiopian Coptic Churches, based on a claim by Origen that Pilate became a Christian in later life and was martyred, have canonised the Governor of Judaea, whose saint's day is June 25.

G. A. Christodoulou, The Knights Templar School, Baldock Hertfordshire

What is the origin of the expression "Perfidious Albion"?

R. Jenkins, Mallorca

It is one of the terms of abuse which the French reserve for us. Others are *les rosbifs*, the "nation of shopkeepers" and *filer à l'anglaise*. "Perfidious Albion" was used, if not coined, by Jacques-Bénigne Bossuet (1627–1704), the bishop who was a polemical supporter of Louis XIV and the scourge of Protestantism.

William Nicoll, Canterbury

In his "First Sermon for the Feast of the Circumcision of Our Lord" Jacques-Bénigne Bossuet wrote: "*L'Angleterre, ah la perfide Angleterre que le rempart de ses mers rendoit inaccessible aux Romains, la foi du Saveur y est abordée.*" "England, ah, faithless England, which the protection afforded by its seas rendered inaccessible to the Romans, the faith of the Saviour spread even there." Perhaps inspired by Bossuet

Augustin, Marquis de Ximénèz (1726–1817) wrote in his poem, *L'Ère des Français,*

> "*Attaquons dans ses eaux*
> *La perfide Albion!*"

"Let us attack in her own waters perfidious Albion!"

The poem gained currency, during the Napoleonic wars, as an invocation to invade England by sea. References to "perfidious Albion" invariably crop up whenever Britain (technically, England) takes action in its national interest and, not surprisingly, at times of Anglo-French tension.

John Cabrera, Grayshott, Surrey

Edward Carson is shown on stage and screen as speaking with an Ulster accent. Yet he was born and educated in Dublin, where he practised for many years. Did he therefore have a Dublin accent?

Nicholas O'Brien, Wotton-under-Edge, Gloucestershire

Despite his role as "uncrowned king of Ulster", Carson was a southerner through and through. Writing about the Oscar Wilde trial, the historian A. T. Q. Stewart speaks of Carson's "plainness of speech, still with its strong Dublin twang", and in referring to Maurice Healy, the Irish barrister and author of *The Old Munster Circuit*, Norman Birkett described himself as "much attracted by [Healy's] brogue although it was slight as compared with Lord Carson".

The stage version may just make Northern Protestants feel more comfortable.

David G. P. Turner QC, London WC1

Some 70 years ago I was invited to play cricket with Lord Carson's son, Ned. While waiting to bat I sat on the grass in front of deckchairs occupied by Lord Carson and a friend and was able to overhear their conversation. He was reminiscing about the time he was summoned during the Home Rule debate by King George V, who then accused him of being a "bloody rebel". His response I gathered was humbly to agree.

As far as I recall, he had no definable accent, though certainly a resonant voice with what was then the normal upper-class intonation.

Murray Hayes, Tealby, Lincolnshire

I have often read that Mussolini made the trains run on time. How did he do this?

Peter Windle, Newcastle upon Tyne

Mussolini was no more capable of getting an efficient rail network running than we are. He ensured that the tiny handful of international trains ran on time by threatening to shoot those responsible if they didn't.

The result was chaos in the rest of the network, as local passenger and freight trains were stopped hours before the international train was due to ensure the latter's swift passage. International passengers and journalists reported the miraculous efficiency — only Italians knew about the disruption everywhere else.

Rainer Burchett, Penrith, Cumbria

When the *Mayflower* sailed from Plymouth in 1620, the 102 people on board were from up to 30 different towns and villages, some as far from Devon as East Anglia and Kent. Who organised the voyage, who were the people recruited, and how was this communicated over the whole of England?

David Peddy, London W9

The core of emigrants was a group of discontented Puritans who had emigrated from Scrooby in Nottinghamshire to the Netherlands in 1608. They settled in Leyden, which had a community of English religious exiles. Finding economic conditions harsh and fearing that their English identity would be lost, they eventually saw the advantages of moving to the newly colonised Americas. There they felt they would be able to raise their standard of living and allowed to pursue their religion peacefully in a wholly English community.

One of the leaders of the Scrooby contingent was William Brewster, who had a connection with Sir Edwin Sandys, the controller of the Virginia Company. Through him they obtained a patent to settle in the company's territory.

To finance the new colony, Brewster and another Scrooby man, William Bradford, entered an agreement with a syndicate of London financiers led by Thomas Weston, who saw the commercial opportunities of trading with the native population. This syndicate hired the *Mayflower* to transport the colonists and brought them over from eyden to England, where they were joined by other emigrants from England, similarly financed by the syndicate.

The expedition leaders hired an English mercenary, Myles Standish, o organise the military protection of the colony. Standish would have been able to answer your question on "facing the music" (see page 35). An officer about to be cashiered was obliged to face a drum party while the charges against him were read out. He was then "drummed out" of the service.

James Hooley, Attleborough, Norfolk

ames Hooley says that William Bradford, one of the Pilgrim Fathers. was from Scrooby in Nottinghamshire. This is not so. He was from Austerfield, near Doncaster, where you will find a William Bradford Avenue in his honour.

Howard Bishop, Fosterhouses, South Yorkshire

Howard Bishop points out that William Bradford was born in "Austerfield, near Doncaster" and not in Scrooby. Austerfield is, in fact, about three miles from Scrooby and much nearer to Scrooby than Doncaster. I suspect that the problem is that Austerfield lies on the other side of the county boundary in Yorkshire.

The Scrooby exiles were a group of people from a number of villages along the old highroad to the North, which is now the A1. William Bradford, who was born in 1590, later came to prominence as the second governor of the Massachussetts Colony in 1621, and remained largely in office until his death in 1657.

James Hooley, Attleborough, Norfolk

What is the largest number of candidates in a by-election, and has any candidate ever recorded zero votes?

Paul Speakman, Manchester

The Newbury by-election on May 6, 1993, had 19 candidates. Working for the BBC at the time, I should know. To meet the provisions of the Representation of the People Act as it applied to broadcasters, we either had to interview all of them for the same programme or none of them. To make things worse, a refusal by any one of them to appear would have meant we could not broadcast the other 18 interviews.

After days of negotiations with all the candidates, including Miss

Whiplash and Screaming Lord Sutch, we succeeded. The rules no longe
apply as the Act was amended before the last general election.

Bruce Parker, Political Editor of BBC South, 1992–200.
Appleshaw, Hampshir

The largest number of candidates in any by-election, which seems t
be 19, is much lower than the largest number of people who applied fo
nomination papers for a single by-election.

That is likely to be the 1963 Rotherham by-election, when at leas
492 applied. Second place would be the Colne Valley by-election at th
same time, when at least 177 applied.

At that time, if any members of the Armed Forces applied to b
candidates, they had to be discharged by the appropriate Service. Th
deposit paid by every candidate was then £150, while the fee levied b
anyone buying themselves out of the Services was much greater. Thu
standing for Parliament was a cheap way of leaving the Services.

Because so many service personnel applied to be candidates, th
rules were changed immediately and a vetting system was introduce
by the Services. This eliminated practically every application.

This method of leaving the Services had been available for som
time. However, it was generally unknown until a magazine published :
story based on characters in the ITV comedy series, *The Army Game*
In this story, Bootsie used this method to try to leave the Army. Whil
the story was fiction, the method was fact, as the "barrack-room
lawyers" soon ascertained.

Robert Steel, Salisbury, Wiltshir

G. T. Harvey polled no votes when standing on a Chartist platform a
Tiverton in 1847.

Matthew Searle, Oxfor

The reputation of a great English radical, George Julian Harney, shoul
not be traduced by the insinuation of unpopularity. Harney, Editor o
the *Northern Star*, stood for Tiverton in the general election of 184
because that was the seat of the Foreign Secretary, Palmerston.

At the hustings he dissected Palmerston's policies in a masterly two
hour speech, and on the show of hands the crowd of 3,000 overwhelm
ingly voted for him. But Harney declined to go to the poll since few i
any of his supporters would have had the vote. Under a democrati

ranchise it would have been Harney, not Palmerston, at the Foreign Office.

David Goodway, University of Leeds

At Ripon, Yorkshire, in December 1860, F. R. Lees (Temperance Charist) obtained zero votes. However, this was at a time when only a minority had the right to vote, making it easier for results such as this.

Since universal franchise, the joint record is held by Lieutenant-Commander Bill Boaks (Public Safety Democratic Monarchist White Resident) at Glasgow Hillhead on March 25, 1982, and Dr Kailish Trivedi (Independent Janata) at Kensington on July 14, 1988. Both obtained just five votes.

Tim Mickleburgh, Grimsby

Did prisoners ever really wear uniforms with arrows on them?
John O'Byrne, Dublin

Until 1877 English and Welsh prisons were run either by the state or by the local authority. The state prisons were few, and received prisoners serving long sentences. They included Dartmoor, Parkhurst, Portland and Chatham. Prisoners in such prisons wore clothes issued by the state, marked as government property by the use of arrows. An arrow has long been a symbol of government property — as anyone in the Armed Forces may recall. Local authority prisons did not mark their kit like this.

All prisons were brought under central government control in 1877, and "arrowed" kit seems to have remained in use, often in those prisons with outdoor "hard labour" parties. Its use was not universal, though — there was no political will to replace all existing stocks throughout the country. Hard labour was abolished in 1948, and with it the last traces of arrowed clothing.

Philip Brookes, Market Drayton, Shropshire

Further to the reply explaining that arrows denoted state property, I believe that the marking of government supplies with broad arrows dates back to 1585 when Sir Philip Sidney became joint master of Ordnance. His personal arms included a "pheon", an heraldic, stylised arrowhead. When military supplies were issued under his control, they were marked accordingly.

David G. P. Chatfield, Rhiw

There has been a great deal of fuss about Britain's sovereignty over Gibraltar. Why has there not been a similar furore over Spain's two enclaves of Ceuta and Melilla in North Africa?

Timothy Blake, Truro, Cornwall

The Spanish Government's case for the retention of the enclaves of Ceuta and Melilla is based on the historical fact that at the time they were captured by the Spanish Crown the Kingdom of Morocco did not exist. For reasons best known to itself, the Moroccan Government is also only luke-warm in its efforts to gain possession over what it regards as colonial possessions.

In the late 1970s, Manuel Fraga Iribarne, the former Ambassador to the Court of St James, set out what would follow, should the Spanish Government ever obtain joint or full sovereignty over Gibraltar. As founder of the post-Franco Partido Popular, he stated that any progress towards the reintegration of Gibraltar into the Spanish state would be offset by a similar reintegration of Ceuta and Melilla into the Moroccan state.

These remarks did not go down well with the electorate and were probably the reason why the election was lost.

The Marques de Lendinez, Fleet, Hampshire

Ceuta and Melilla have been declared by Spain to be an integral part of Spain; Gibraltar has not been declared by the UK to be an integral part of it. Under the 1713 Treaty of Utrecht, Spain has "first refusal" should Britain decide to leave the Rock. Spain has been trying to get the UN Decolonisation Commission to declare Gibraltar a colony which should be decolonised, so that Britain would have to withdraw and Spain pick up on an area that is geographically part of Spain.

For Britain, Gibraltar is now not nearly so important as it was, and would be quite happy to hand over the area. It is also acutely embarrassed that the Gibraltarians want to remain British. As London would gladly get rid of Northern Ireland, so it much prefers good relations with Madrid to hanging on to a few acres of rock and for a thousand British citizens.

Professor A. E. Alcock, Ulster University, Coleraine, Co Londonderry

Spain demands that the British return the Rock to them, and simply refuses to listen to any complaints regarding their ownership of Ceuta and Melilla. It was, however, happy to mobilise most of its army in order to protect a rocky outcrop (supposedly part of Spain) inhabited by 12 goats when Moroccan forces set foot upon it last year.

Hugo Soul, Sherborne, Dorset

Ceuta was conquered by the Portuguese in 1415, not the Spanish. Between 1580 and 1640 Portugal was occupied by what we, in Portugal, describe as "the Philips". When we regained independence in 1640 Ceuta remained Spanish.

Paulo Lowndes Marques, Lisbon

How much was the original king's ransom?

Lawrence Frewin, London SW12

Returning from the Third Crusade, Richard I was taken prisoner by Duke Leopold of Austria, who sought to exact a price for handing his royal captive over to the German emperor, Henry VI. After great efforts by his mother, Queen Eleanor of Aquitaine, Richard I was released in 1194 in return for a ransom of 150,000 silver marks (or £100,000): 100,000 marks to the emperor and 50,000 to the duke.

Leopold was excommunicated for daring to imprison a crusader and died the same year.

Jennifer Miller, London SW15

John II, King of France, was captured by the English at Poitiers in 1356 and his ransom set at four million gold crowns, reduced in 1358 to three million. He was released under the terms of the Treaty of Brétigny in 1360 in exchange for his son, the Duke of Anjou.

David II, King of Scotland, was captured at the Battle of Neville's Cross in 1346. Of 100,000 marks demanded by the English, less than a quarter was paid.

Dilys Firn, Liverpool

If the Americans had not got involved in the Second World War, what would have happened?

Peter Cahill-Shaw, Milton Keynes

Three outcomes in three global areas might be speculated. In Europe, the major action from 1943 onwards would have been a westward moving Eastern Front, as the Soviet Union wore Germany down by attrition. Because of the loss of British and French material left after Dunkirk, it would have taken the resources of Britain and the Empire until the early 1950s to have launched a second front in continental Europe. Without American involvement, such an invasion would not have been viable before, in the late 1940s, Europe's Eastern and Western fronts had merged at the Atlantic coast, possibly then including Soviet domination of Great Britain and Eire.

Without the involvement of the US, the war in the Far East would not have ended in the use of atomic bombs, and Japanese expansion on the western Pacific rim would have seen the permanent loss of British influence in South East Asia and Australasia. In Africa, Germany's forces, constantly being reduced to provide manpower for the Soviet war, would have succumbed to British and Empire forces.

So, four large power blocks might have emerged: the British Empire of Africa, the Soviet Empire of Western Asia and Europe, the Japanese Empire of Eastern Asia and the Pacific, and American dominance in the Western hemisphere.

Stephen Gray, Hurstpierpoint, Sussex

Britain would probably have had to sue for peace and accept terms favourable to Germany. Communism would eventually have collapsed and the British Empire would have disintegrated.

Germany and Japan would have become economic and industrial superpowers. Britain's industrial base would have declined. Prestigious motor car marques such as Rolls-Royce and Bentley would have moved into German ownership. Under Hitler's dream of a unified Europe, the Continent would have been controlled by an unelected central body. There would be a single currency controlled by a central bank in Germany, probably somewhere like Frankfurt.

Britain would be divided into its constituent countries with pseudo-parliaments for Wales, Scotland and Northern Ireland. England would be split into "regions" monitored by the central body. Britain's laws would be subservient to those laid down by the central body.

Not a pretty picture! Thank heavens the Americans did enter the war.

Mike Hughes, Wetherby, West Yorkshire

Sprechen Sie Deutsch?

Marc Cox, Wolverhampton

4. SCIENCE MATTERS

Is it true that water going down a plughole will swirl in either a clockwise or anti-clockwise motion depending on whether it is in the northern or the southern hemisphere?

John Morrison, Keighley, West Yorkshire

The phenomenon which causes an apparent force to be felt in different directions on moving bodies in the northern and southern hemispheres is the Coriolis effect, which is due to the rotation of the Earth (named after the French mathematician, Gustave Gaspard Coriolis, 1792–1843).

Although the Coriolis effect is often taught in schools as causing the water to swirl different ways down sinks and loos, the effect is actually quite weak on small scales, and will not have any effect upon the average bath. The currents remaining in a sink, bath or loo from the filling process are much more powerful than the Coriolis effect, and unless you leave your body of water for a number of days until all these currents have subsided, the water will tend to swirl out the plug hole in the direction of filling. Therefore, the use of the hot or cold tap and the shape of the bowl will primarily decide the draining rotation.

The Coriolis effect is best observed in weather systems, which are much larger and much more affected by the motion of the Earth through friction over many thousands of square kilometres. Low pressure systems in the northern hemisphere rotate counter-clockwise, and in the southern hemisphere they rotate clockwise.

Will Smith, London SW15

The answer to this question is simple: try it! Out of five attempts, the water in my sink emptied clockwise twice and anti-clockwise three times, so it isn't true.

Many people who watched Michael Palin's excellent series *Pole To Pole* will remember seeing a very convincing demonstration performed at the Equator by a man with a basin full of swirling water. The water appeared to rotate in one direction as he walked towards the line of the Equator, lose its spin over the line and then rotate in the opposite direction as the line was crossed.

Apparently this is a very lucrative trick performed for tourists and the BBC forgot to check the authenticity of the demonstration. (See Philip Plait's book *Bad Astronomy: Misconceptions and Misuses Revealed*.)

Jeanette Stafford, Glasgow

Further to your previous respondents, who state that this is not true in the case of a small sink, bath or loo, the definitive answer was provided in the late 1950s by engineers working at MIT.

They built a large, wide, cylindrical tank with a small drain hole in the centre of its base. The tank was filled with water, and the water allowed to settle until it was at rest in the laboratory, a procedure which took about three days. The drain valve was then opened and a swirling motion developed. The experiment was repeated many times and it was found that the swirl was always in the same anticlockwise direction.

The engineers did not move their apparatus to the southern hemisphere. Instead, they arranged the hose used to fill the tank so that, after filling and a shorter period of settling, the water was gently rotating in the opposite direction to that observed in their earlier experiments. When the drain valve was opened, the contrived rotation gradually slowed down to zero and then reversed.

The explanation of the phenomenon is that when the contents of the tank are at rest, they are in fact rotating with the Earth in space. The particles of fluid nearer the Equator move faster than those nearer the poles. As the water flows towards the drain hole its moment of momentum is conserved and the tangential component of its velocity is increased, thus setting up the vortex which is observed. The effect is greatest at the poles and zero at the Equator, and in a carefully controlled experiment the vortex rotation is anticlockwise in the northern hemisphere and clockwise in the southern hemisphere.

Ray Franklin, Oxford

Why, when listening to a mechanical clock, do we always perceive the sound sequence to be "tick/tock" and not "tock/tick", which logically it should be in 50 per cent of random observations?

Robert Griffin, Bristol

We don't strictly perceive "tick/tock", since the sound of every tick is the same. The brain tends to impose a pattern on even an identical series of sounds. There seems to be a universal tendency — and not only in English — for the first member of such pairs to have a high front close vowel such as "i" and the second a low back open vowel like "o" or "a". Consider: chit-chat, bric-a-brac, flip-flop, mish-mash and fiddle-faddle.

Ormond Uren, London NW5

Every tick is not necessarily the same, since the mechanical escapement is not symmetrical, and the amount that the escapement wheel is allowed to progress is often different on the left swing of the pendulum from that on the right swing. Hence, one tick is heavier than the other. Furthermore, if the clock is not set precisely level, the interval between successive ticks may not be the same, giving tick/tock, tick/tock (or tock/tick, tock/tick).

G. H. May, Guisborough

Why are the numbers on telephone keypads arranged with 1 at top left and 9 at bottom right while on computers and calculators 1 is bottom left and 9 top right? In both cases 0 is at the bottom.

Mike Read, Bicester

Evolution! The dial telephone transmitted a series of pulses indicating the required digit (one pulse for 1, two pulses for 2, and so on). Since "no pulses" would have been equivalent to "nothing happening", zero was represented by ten pulses (and the exchanged wiring adjusted accordingly).

Mechanical adders were actuated by a rack-and-pinion mechanism where the distance travelled by the rack was proportional to the value of the depressed key, further movement being inhibited by the top of the rack butting up against a projection on the key. Since the rack movement was in the direction away from the user (to keep the adding mechanism conveniently in sight), low numbers were at the bottom and zero, which prevented any movment at all, was before one. The electronics age need not have perpetuated these traditions but it has.

Eric Huggins, Southwold, Suffolk

Who created the first pair of spectacles, and where and when were they first worn in public?

Warwick Hood, London SW8

The Roman statesman Seneca, born around 4BC, is said to have read books by looking through a "glass globe". The Emperor Nero (AD54–68) used emerald gem lenses to view gladiatorial games, and they became a fashion accessory among the patrician class.

Eyeglasses were introduced in Italy in the 14th century by Alessandro di Spina of Florence, and also appeared in China at around the same time.

John O'Byrne, Dublin

Rock crystals probably used as lenses have been found in Egypt in a site dated to 2600BC. Magnifying lenses have been used throughout history — Seneca, as your previous correspondent pointed out, read through a water bowl, for example.

The first recorded use of spectacles was in Italy in the 1280s — a monastic text in 1306 referred to "it being 20 years since the coming of this great benefit".

From this text we can infer that spectacles had come into general use. Before then, one-off spectacle frames may have been made to order for individuals. A number of people in 13th-century Italy claimed the invention but since lenses had been used since antiquity the novelty lay in putting two lenses together and perching them on the nose with a clip — not exactly rocket science. Thus it would be hard to identify who precisely could be credited with the idea.

The first spectacle wearers were probably Venetians in about 1285. However, spectacle frames were heavy and clumsy until the 18th century, so though there are many illustrations of people reading with spectacles in their own homes, there are few of people wearing spectacles in the street.

Russell Vallance, London SE18

From the 13th century, nose spectacles did not feature sides and had to be held in place with the hand or perched precariously on the face, relying on the tensile qualities of the material from which the frame was made. The lenses they contained were useful primarily to literate presbyopics (usually aged over 40 — an advanced age for the period), so not many would have been seen being worn in public before the mid-14th century.

The London optician Edward Scarlett advertised spectacles as we would know them (with sides to rest on the temples) only at the surprisingly late date of c.1730.

One of the first men who would have been able to wear such spectacles was Dr Johnson but he was on record as refusing to be seen wearing them in public and there are no known pictures of him with them on.

Neil Handley, BOA Museum Curator, The College of
Optometrists, London WC2

If two dogs of the same breed meet each other in the street, does each recognise the other as being of the same breed, or as just another dog?

Roy Cookson, Manchester

We walk our two Newfoundland PAT (Pets as Therapy) dogs, Charlie and Pilot, around Crufts and Discover Dogs at Earls Court and they meet literally thousands of different and varied breeds of dogs. It is only when they see and meet another Newfoundland do they get very excited and give a happy bark of greeting.

Nick and Sandra Oliver, Cambridge

Dogs do recognise their own breed in the street, but my two Pug bitches are remarkably cognisant: they recognised the televised image of the male dog who won the Pug Best Of Breed at Crufts.

The two bitches were dozing quietly while a number of other dogs were shown, but when the Pug best of breed appeared, both bitches leapt up at the television, stood up on their hind legs and covered the screen with wet puggie kisses, wailing with pleasure and waving their tails enthusiastically. When the picture moved to other breeds, Rosie and Bella returned to their evening sleep and took no more interest.

Kay White, Chichester, West Sussex

My four-year-old racing whippet, Merlin, definitely recognises dogs of other breeds, shrieking and lunging as they approach. Top of his list of pet hates are collies, followed by black labradors and small terriers. However, if we meet a whippet or greyhound, he is his usual charming self.

L. J. Rankin, Tewkesbury, Gloucestershire

Do wasps and bees ever fight each other? Are they involved in "gang warfare"? Or do they recognise each other as distant cousins?

Paul A. Smith, Sheffield

Yes, they do. As a beekeeper, I regard wasps as ruthless marauders: their need for sugar towards the end of the summer motivates them to make every effort to get into a beehive and rob its honey harvest.

Guard bees at the entrance can usually keep them out, but if there is a small opening elsewhere in the hive, wasps invade, and the bees defend. As bees die when they sting, they fight to the death, and the result can be a hive bereft not only of honey but also most of its bees. Disaster!

Ann Procter, Somerton, Somerset

Why, as one gets older, does the passage of time seem to accelerate?

Richard Gardner, York

Consciousness, as humans understand it, is a quality related to time. Consciousness relates constantly, not simply to the present moment, such as an animal might, but to its entire span of existence. Human beings are the only creatures who have "documentary" memories, ie, we remember events in words and images.

For most people this "reference" to our individual history is a constant activity of the mind, which refers, in the unconsious, to its beginnings. We are also the only creatures who are able to be aware of the certainty that this life will end. This means that each section of our day, week, year, lifetime, is lived out as some kind of "increment", not of "clock" time, but of these mysterious "increments of consciousness" which cover events, like a family holiday. a dinner party, one's schooldays, a war, and so on, in that "periodic" way.

This means that some kind of proportionality is subconsciously at work, so that a year in the life of a two-year-old is one half of his lifetime, where the same time would be only one-hundredth part of the life of a centenarian. These "units of consciousness" are therefore, lived out proportionally, constantly referring to the beginnings of that consciousness. Each day, month, year, then, seems to be a shorter and shorter period, as we get older, simply because it becomes, proportionally, a smaller and smaller part of our lifetime.

Norman Mackenzie, London E11

This illusion is caused by the fact that what is left of one's life is rapidly diminishing. It can be compared to drinking a nice bottle of wine. When you start, it seems to go very slowly, with plenty left to enjoy. But when you are three-quarters of the way down, the rest seems to go very quickly indeed!

Dennis May, London Ell

I have always believed this happens because the brain gradually slows down. Not only do days, weeks, months and years fly past at ever increasing speed, but films, symphonies and similar experiences seem much shorter than they did in our youth. The pity is that books take longer to read, but perhaps we enjoy them more.

Dennis Palmer (aged 74), Shrewsbury

Time is rather like water draining from a sink: the nearer it gets to the centre the quicker it spins until, like us, it disappears from view.

Bernard Parke, Guildford, Surrey

The cognitive mechanism by which we perceive time is a function of our awareness of our successive experiences. When we first become self-aware, all our experiences are new, and they register in our aware-ness accordingly. With the passage of time this factor decreases. Most of our experiences become repetitions, and our daily lives contain larger stretches of routine activities. For practical reasons these become fil-tered out from our awareness, and so register in it less, and sometimes not at all. After a bit, much of our habitual day is lived on cognitive autopilot. This is why you are sometimes not sure whether you have locked the door or closed the window and have to go back and check.

However, this process is not directly dependent on ageing, and is reversible. When you are travelling through a foreign country where all experiences are new, few activities are routine, everything is differ-ent, and each day unlike the others, time seems to slow down. So you might say: "I can't believe it's only a week ago we left Boulogne. It seems more like a month." When you eventually get home, someone stuck there in the meantime might remark: "Are you back already? You've only just left."

Dr Michael Senior, Colwyn Bay, Clwyd

Why does the old (northbound) Blackwall Tunnel under the

Thames have so many bends in it? Why couldn't they have just tunnelled straight across?

Jim Turner, Sevenoaks, Kent

Both the old Blackwall Tunnel and the Rotherhithe Tunnel to its west have bends at both ends as a precaution against the horses (old-fashioned cars) becoming spooked or overexcited by the light at the end of the tunnel, and bolting.

Graham Pexton, London SE8

Under-river tunnels are one of the more difficult parts of the civil engineer's repertoire. The line of a tunnel is a compromise between keeping the under-river section short, since this is the deepest and most risky section to construct, while finding sites for the intermediate shafts, and bringing the approaches up with sufficient length to limit the gradients, and to emerge where they will connect to an existing road network.

Ground conditions under the lower Thames are poor with loose, waterlogged ground. Marc Brunel's Thames Tunnel (1825–43) between Wapping and Rotherhithe was an heroic feat, at great cost. Later railways avoided tunnelling under the river.

In contrast, the early deep Tube railways were driven through the London clay, considered an excellent tunnelling medium. By the 1880s a new technique, using compressed air to keep water out of deep foundations, became available, and in 1890 the new London County Council asked for reports on the first under-river tunnels being built in this way under the Hudson River (New York) and between Canada and the US at Sarnia.

The LCC designed the Blackwall Tunnel to use these new techniques (built 1892–97), and employed the same contractor, Pearson, as for the Hudson River Tunnel. A clay blanket was laid on the riverbed over the line of the tunnel to prevent the compressed air "blowing out". Like any prudent engineer using new techniques, they minimised their problems with straight tunnel drives between the four shafts, and the four kinks were no problem for contemporary horse-drawn traffic.

In later years, soft ground tunnelling, developing fast with the growth of the deep Underground, gained the ability to build curved tunnels, and so the bends in later tunnels, while still numerous, are not so apparent.

Chris Bradfield, Henfield, West Sussex

Why, when I am trying to concentrate on some difficult task, do I find my tongue sticking out?

Paul Rayner, Bridlington, East Yorkshire

I find that sticking my tongue out stops me dribbling.

It also appears that the extent of this protrusion is in direct proportion to the complexity of the task being undertaken.

Roy Haycock, Tunbridge Wells, Kent

A former girlfriend of mine did it even in her mid-forties because she said that it stopped her from swearing or talking when reading or concentrating. It was slightly disdainful but quite endearing.

Children who are too old to suck their thumbs legitimately do it as a less obvious and more discreet alternative to the external equivalent. This could be either a form of security or simply a means of self-control, as seen in the hands praying position.

Musicians, particularly horn players, do it in anticipation of the next note to be played after a rest.

The village idiot in Fada N'Gorma, Upper Volta (now Burkina Faso), did it repeatedly when I spent four days among the Hausa people in 1981. Sami visited us daily, always with his tongue firmly between his teeth and lips. When I asked why, I was told that he was closer to God than us so his behaviour was above criticism.

Tim Boddington, Byfield, Northamptonshire

Why do joints "click" when the finger is pulled?

Mark Russell, Kirkcaldy, Fife

Pulling the finger joint apart causes it to click because of the suddenly reduced pressure in the joint's natural lubricant, the synovial fluid. This reduction causes the quantity of air within the fluid to come out of solution (rather like a bottle of fizzy water suddenly being opened) and to form minute bubbles. When the joint is released, these bubbles suddenly collapse and cause the sharp click. This phenomenon is known to mechanical engineers as "cavitation".

The party trick must not be played too often. The damage caused to the joint's natural bearing material, the cartilage, should the bubbles collapse near its surface, is irreparable and is a cause of arthritis.

Philip Economou, Rugby

"Cavitation", described by Philip Economou as the source of joint clicks, was well described and informative. I was puzzled, though, to read his observation that overdoing this party trick could lead to the development of arthritis.

As a rheumatologist, I see many youngsters and their parents who fear that joint clicking indicates the onset of (juvenile) arthritis. Much time is spent reassuring them that this is not the case. I am not aware of any evidence to support your correspondent's statement and I suggest that joint clicking is entirely harmless.

Another sound, "crepitus", may arise from joints in established arthritis, but this is a consequence, not a cause.

David James, Diana, Princess of Wales Hospital, Grimsby

When camouflage is the name of the game, why do fleeing rabbits signal up a very visible white rump?

Denis Roche, Droitwich, Worcestershire

Rabbits have alternative escape mechanisms. One is to freeze; this is effective only (and not always) against airborne predators; the other is to run into a hole that (the rabbit hopes) will be too small for the predator. Natural selection presumably strengthens the survival rate of the canniest and fastest rabbits. If the leading animal has a white rump, the less canny presumably find it easier to follow, so increasing a genetic tendency towards speed, canniness and white rumps.

Anne Malins, Colchester

This was once a favourite counter to Darwin's theory of "the survival of the fittest". Surely, it was said, the conspicuous rabbit would be chased and caught more easily? Yet his fellows would see the rump as warning of the peril, and flee to safety. So it would save many for the loss of one.

Rabbits breed very quickly and just one could pass the genes to very many. Colonies with even one such distant early-warning device would suffer fewer losses through predation. Any new breakaway colonies from them would fail more quickly if none reproduced it; by a process of refinement through gradual loss of such colonies only rabbits carrying the genes for it were left, so all rabbits have it.

Christopher Nutt, Cambridge

Rabbits will also drum their hind feet with audible thumpings to sound an alarm if danger is perceived, and that, like the white flash of its scut as it bolts, is a signal to other rabbits near by. Our roe, red and sika deer flare out a bright white caudal patch as they run from danger, and the North American whitetail deer erects a very long, bright, silvery-white tail almost like a flag. Pigs, wild and domesticated, flee noisily with tails held vertical.

Animals are programmed through evolution to try to preserve and perpetuate the genes of their own kind. As Tennyson said in *In Memoriam* (1850):

So careful of the type she seems,
So careless of the single life.

Colin McKelvie, Culbokie, Ross-shire

Why is it impossible to concentrate on reading something when someone within earshot is using a mobile telephone? This is not usually the case if people near by are engaged in normal conversation.

David Horton, Slough

We are asked why these are distracting to involuntary eavesdroppers. Two factors contribute: a) speakers on mobile phones usually talk over-loudly and b) one half of a conversation tempts the hearer to try to invent the missing half and this endeavour is an attention grabber.

The reason why speakers on mobiles talk loudly is in major part because these phones have low or no side-tone — ie, you cannot hear your own voice so you speak more loudly because of the impression that your voice is "getting lost in the ether". They also have acousti-cally unshielded microphones unlike old-style wired phones which gives the same impression of talking into space. Lastly, people believe that mobiles are marginal devices in terms of transmission quality so you shout (usually quite unnecessarily nowadays) to make sure you are heard at the far end.

This last point demonstrates a counterproductive feedback effect. If you talk quietly to someone they will tend to speak back to you loudly and vice versa. But if you talk loudly they will speak less loudly and you will subjectively speak even more loudly.

Michael Forrest, Henley-on-Thames

Why can I happily read on a train or aeroplane, but put me in a car or bus and I feel sick within seconds of starting to read?

John Wilcock, Harpenden, Hertfordshire

"Sensory conflict" is the accepted theory for the genesis of travel, or motion, sickness. This states that if sensory signals are not in the expected combination, then nausea can occur. When you are reading in a car, there is no relative movement between the words on the page and the eyes and so the visual scene does not appear to move. However, the balance organs (the vestibular system) sense the motion of the vehicle. Therefore, the visual and balance senses are in conflict. In a car or bus, there are repeated accelerations, such as speeding up, slowing down and going round corners. These accelerations are easily sensed by the balance organs and so a compelling sensory conflict can easily occur. However, in a train or aeroplane the accelerations do not occur so often or with as much vigour and their characteristics are not as easily sensed, so the conflict is not so strong.

To stop getting sick, one answer is to minimise the sensory conflict. In a car or bus this inevitably means avoiding reading. Also, the driver can help. They should drive smoothly on winding roads or urban streets to minimise the sensation of motion. Children might be better occupied with a story recorded on to tape, rather than reading a book or playing a handheld game. The car driver almost never gets motion sickness. So it is often a good idea to let the most susceptible traveller drive, especially on winding roads.

Dr Neil Mansfield, Department of Human Sciences, Loughborough University

The practice of bleeding the sick for almost any complaint was practised for several centuries. Was it ever successful, and when was it discredited?

Ron Lee, Kettering, Northamptonshire

Blood-letting, or "therapeutic phlebotomy", was a feature of medical treatment going back to Ancient Greece, China and India. In Europe it was incorporated in many medical belief systems ranging from the texts of Galen in classical times to medieval and Renaissance astrology. Quite large amounts of blood could be removed in some treatments — up to one third of a normal adult's supply. The removal of blood stimulates the body to produce new blood cells. For a few days the proportion of new cells in the bloodstream is unnaturally high and the oxygen content of the blood is correspondingly increased. This gives a feeling of vitality and wellbeing. However, it does not treat any illnesses.

The new-style "Paris Medicine" of the early 1800s questioned traditional practices, and Pierre Louis demonstrated that blood-letting had no effect on outcomes in pneumonia and fever cases. Weakened patients could be harmed: George Washington, for example, in December 1799 had nine pints of blood removed within 24 hours and died shortly after. Despite Louis's work, blood-letting continued as a medical practice well into the 1840s in Europe and is still used in some traditional treatments in India.

In Western medicine small-scale blood-letting through the use of medical leeches has enjoyed a revival in recent years as a means of drawing a blood supply through delicate injured tissues.

Russell Vallance, London SE18

I have polycythaemia (too many red blood cells), and have been bled, beneficially, every six weeks for several years.

David Bowsher, Liverpool

When firearms are released skywards (as at Palestinian funerals) is there a danger of the bullets falling down to earth and harming anybody? Has anyone ever been killed or injured in such a way?

Edward West, London W6

Falling bullets have killed countless people when firearms have been wantonly discharged skywards. But the level of risk depends on the elevation at which the shot ascends and descends.

A bullet fired perpendicularly eventually stalls and begins to descend at a speed dictated by gravity but mitigated by air resistance. Its peak or "terminal" velocity is reached long before it hits the ground, and the impact energy of a typical military rifle bullet falling thus is unlikely to cause more than bruising.

Maximum distance of bullet travel, with the projectile retaining sufficient energy to kill or seriously wound at ground level, occurs when a rifle cartridge is discharged at an angle of around 30 degrees. With modern military ammunition the potentially lethal range is between two and three miles.

Colin McKelvie, Culbokie, Ross-shire

The English war novelist Wilfred Ewart, who served in the Scots Guards 1914–18 and survived the battles of Neuve Chapelle, Ypres, the Somme, Passchendaele, Cambrai and Arras was killed on his hotel balcony in Mexico City on New Year's Eve 1922 by a spent bullet from the sky, fired by someone celebrating the holiday in the streets. The bullet hit him in the eye.

Mike Horsman, Tewin, Hertfordshire

In P. J. O'Rourke's dispatches from the Gulf War, as contained in his book *Give War a Chance* (1992), he commented that in the wake of the liberation of Kuwait City, Kuwaiti soldiers spent the best part of six days firing every available weapon into the air, including the heavy mounted machine guns on their armoured personnel carriers.

"It's one thing to get plinked on the head by a falling pistol bullet," says O'Rourke, "but a .50-caliber slug plummeting from the sky at terminal velocity could go right through to the soles of your feet. One American marine told me that sixteen people had been killed by 'happy fire' so far, but a US Army officer said it was more like a hundred and fifty."

Dominic Bescoby, Sheffield

This is a common means of celebration by the Latino immigrant community in East Los Angeles. Dozens of people have been killed and injured here on New Year's Eve and Cinco de Mayo (Mexican Independence Day) in the past two decades, prompting a gunfire awareness programme by the City Council to warn people that what goes up, must come down.

Neil Fletcher, Los Angeles

If the Sun were suddenly extinguished, how long could life on Earth continue?

Gemma Beech, York

The Sun is just another star and it won't last forever, but it will be around for millions of years yet. It will either explode in a supernova, which would probably destroy the Earth, or else implode, becoming a black hole which would then suck the Earth in.

Maureen Robinson, Belfast

Astronomers are confident that the Sun will not explode as a supernova, simply because it is too small a mass; nor will it become a black hole through implosion or any other means. Even if it did become a black hole, the Earth would not be "sucked in" because the gravitation due to a black hole is exactly the same as from any ordinary star.

But suppose the Sun was somehow mysteriously "switched off"? The Earth's surface receives almost all its heat from the Sun, with only a relatively small amount from radioactivity in the Earth's interior or from other sources in space. But the rocks and seas store a great deal of heat, and it would take some time for the surface to get too cold for life. After a few weeks, there would be wintry conditions in many places, and after a month or two it would start to snow in the tropics. Rivers and lakes would freeze. All food supplies rely on photosynthesis in plants, so the cycle of crops and the food chain would break down, and mass starvation would take place as soon as stored food supplies ran out.

The oceans would freeze, and gradually the ice would solidify all the way to the sea bed; it has to give up a lot of stored heat for this to happen. After many years the heat stored in the water would finally be radiated away, the very air itself would cool and liquefy, then freeze. At this point, with a few exceptions such as strange life forms huddled around volcanic vents on the sea floor, all other life on Earth would cease. After a few millennia passed, the surface of the Earth would approach equilibrium with the cosmic background radiation and internal radioactivity, with only the occasional volcano to break the frozen silence.

Mike Dworetsky, Stanmore, Middlesex

Who first "rubbed salt in the wound"? Was it ever a good idea?
Chris Sharpe, Ilfracombe, Devon

The expression "rubbing salt in the wound" means to make things worse. Yet rubbing salt into a wound, albeit painful, is a good, if crude, means of cleaning the wound of harmful bacteria.

I remember a history master telling us some forty years ago of a skirmish in the Napoleonic wars where the British were caught off guard swimming (in the nude).

After beating off the French, they observed that the British wounds healed much more quickly and cleanly than usual. The absence of probably extremely dirty clothes perhaps helped, along with the salt water.

Dr Peter B. Baker, London W5

When corporal punishment by flogging still existed in the Royal Navy it was usual for the victim's back to be rubbed with salt. This was intended to speed healing of the lacerations — and it may have succeeded, but it certainly made the pain worse.

Michael Sandford, Aberyscir, Breconshire

I can confirm that it is an excellent, if painful, idea. Some 20 years ago, on a day's leave from my ship in Haifa, I decided to go swimming in the Dead Sea. This contains 25.5 per cent of dissolved salts, mainly sodium chloride. By contrast, sea water in the world's oceans has an average salinity of 3.5 per cent of dissolved salts, again mostly, but not entirely, sodium chloride or table salt. Swimming on your front in the Dead Sea is not to be recommended as any splashes of the water in the eyes are very painful, while swimming on your back means you cannot see where you are going. In the latter mode I swam into some pillars of crystallised salt in shallow water and grazed my back quite badly. The pain of the initial grazes and the sting of the salt in the wounds was impressive, but I was equally impressed by the speed with which the wounds healed: less than a week. The use of this procedure might not be popular with patients, but the application of anything with a high osmotic value, such as cane syrup or honey, will have the same effect in killing the bacteria by drying them out. Incidentally after flogging in the Royal Navy, salt was not rubbed in the wounds, they were repeatedly washed with sea water.

Dr Robert M. Bruce-Chwatt Ship's Surgeon, 1985–90

When the late Sir Archibald McIndoe was treating burnt airmen in the Battle of Britain, he noted that those shot down into the sea reacted more favourably than those coming down on land. Thus he instituted the warm saline bath treatment for dressing burns at East Grinstead, a regimen which continued for some 30 years.

Ronald Brown, Chichester

If the world were suddenly to stop spinning, what effect would it have on us?

Peter Rushforth, Bradford, West Yorkshire

At the equator, you would suddenly be thrown west at about 1,000mph, the rotational speed of the Earth. In the UK, this speed would have reduced to 600mph. At the North and South poles, however, the sudden disappearance of rotation would probably induce a mild feeling of giddiness.

M. J. Piff, Sheffield

The Earth rotates from west to east so, contrary to the earlier answer, someone at the Equator would be thrown eastward at about 1,000 mph.

John Chambers, Tadworth, Surrey

In H. G. Wells's short story, *The Man Who Could Work Miracles*, the world abruptly stops spinning — with the result that everything and every person on its surface is violently hurled about. Most of mankind would die in such circumstances. Wells does not mention the miles-high tsunamis that would be generated by the world's oceans. But I assume the questioner is really asking about a world that simply did not rotate at all.

During the course of a year, each part of the Earth would experience the equivalent of a single day as it orbited the Sun. For several months there would be continuous night, and almost all vegetation would die, leading to universal starvation.

During the long day and night, temperatures would become intolerably high and then low. No rotation would mean no Coriolis forces and hence no wind-driven weather systems. The air on the daylight side of the Earth would become saturated with water vapour but rain might not occur at all. As night approached the atmospheric cooling might lead to continuous snow for months.

The rotation of the Earth is thought to influence movement in the solid iron core and the molten iron layer above it, creating the Earth's magnetic field which protects us from lethal solar radiation. If the world did not spin there might be no magnetic field, so everyone might die from radiation rather than starvation.

B. P. J. White, Ashford, Middlesex

It would improve our test match prospects no end. Every other country has great spinners, whereas England hasn't produced a decent spinner for decades.

Eddie Curran, Middlesbrough

Tony would have to go.

Edward Young, Reading

Life on Earth would cease to exist without the Sun, but what would be the effect on life on Earth if the Moon were somehow to vanish from the sky?

Anne Pearson, Glasgow

The Moon is largely responsible for the ebb and flow of ocean tides, allowing seawater to form pools, which are thought to be where life originated on Earth some four billion years ago.

The Moon is also believed to be responsible for the stability of the Earth's axis and this has a direct bearing on our seasons. Without this stabilising factor, the Earth would develop a very different climate that would produce significant temperature variations within the year. It might even make life on Earth impossible.

Grant Woodruff, High Wycombe

The overriding importance of the Sun being self-evident, a (fictitious) Russian philosopher by the name of Prutkov is quoted by P. E. Cleator in his book *Into Space* (1953) as insisting: "Of the Sun and Moon, the Moon is plainly the more important, as it provides us with light when it is dark and most needed, whereas the Sun appears only in the daytime, when it is light anyhow."

Michael White, Malvern, Worcestershire

In the same way that a ballerina can increase her spin rate by withdrawing her arms and her extended leg, the Earth would rotate faster without the influence of the Moon.

Our planet is slowing down because of the Moon's influence and the Moon in turn is orbiting us quicker. As a result, we would have shorter days and gravity would appear to have weakened. Soon night workers would be going to work in daytime, and plants, as well as our offspring, would be towering above us.

Peter Milner, Weston Colville, Cambridgeshire

Can a person blind from birth dream visually? If so, what does he or she see?

Rudi Leavor, Bradford, West Yorkshire

It all depends if you subscribe to the blank slate theory of mind that is currently being challenged (albeit in a different context) or the Platonic ideal theory.

Blank slate states that a person is born without any concepts — and prejudices — of the world. Therefore, a blind person can only dream things that s(he) visualised in the mind's eye by other senses. Whereas, if the ideal is imprinted, the dream can be similar to that of a non-blind person. For example, horses all differ slightly but we all know a horse when we see one.

Eser Utku, Istanbul

A person blind from birth does not experience visual dreams. The reason for this is that visual dreaming involves the same area of the visual cerebral cortex, at the back of the brain, as conscious vision. It takes time for the cortex to become attuned to the signals it is receiving and in the case of vision it appears that this process may not be complete at less than four years or so. Thus, a child becoming blind at two years of age, for example, also may not dream visually, the attunement time being too short. See an article by Geoffrey A. Hocker in the *Journal of the Royal Society of Medicine*, Vol 96, February 2003.

Dr A. G. White, London W1

My attention has been drawn by a sighted friend to your last answer, which was read to me. As someone blind from birth, I should like to reply as follows:

I hear, smell, feel and touch in my dreams, but I do not see. It may be, as Dr White, suggests, that the visual cortex is not sufficiently developed and that is the reason, but might I also suggest that a person blind from birth has no visual memory and this too is a reason for non-visual dreams.

By way of example, my mother died some five years ago. I never saw my mother. Consequently, when I had a dream about her recently, I could hear her talking to me, I felt her hand, heard her footsteps and, though she had given up smoking long before her death, I could smell a cigarette so definitely that when I woke, I really thought she was back with me. At no point during my dream did I see her.

Mary Phillips, Sutton, Surrey

Should I be swallowed by a whale, Jonah-style, what would be my chances of survival?

Dan Mewse, Exmouth, Devon

There is a mistake in the translation of the book of Jonah: he was swallowed by a "big fish" not a whale. Traditional Jewish sources explain that the fish involved was a Leviathan, which is mentioned in the book of Job. As a question of practicalities, I don't think that there is any whale that would prevent a human from suffocating in its belly if it were to swallow one whole.

Harvey Green, London

Whales are supposed to live only on krill, which they take in through their filter-like teeth. The throat is too small to ingest any larger creature. However, in the old whaling town of Eden in South Australia, there is a story of a whaler falling overboard whilst whaling, and being swallowed by a right whale. A short time afterwards the whale was caught and the man was saved. However, his hair had turned white — as had his skin, which had also become wrinkled. He was found to be blind.

Bernard Parke, Guildford, Surrey

A distant relative of mine, James Bartley, is reputed to have been swallowed by a whale off the Falkland Islands in 1891. He was the captain of a whaling ship. The whale had been harpooned and was being tied to the side of the boat when it thrashed, causing Bartley and some of his crew to fall into the sea.

The whale eventually died and was towed to Port Stanley for processing. When it was cut open, horrified workers found Bartley in the whale's throat, still alive. Apparently his skin was bleached white from the reflux acid of the whale. What happened to him subsequently is not known. Some say that he died shortly after the event, others say that he retired to a nursing home in Shropshire.

Richard Bartley, Henllan, Denbighshire

Slightly better than that of the whale.

Edward Jenkins, Llandre, West Wales

For how long, after beheading, is consciousness maintained?
Julian Neely, Horsham, West Sussex

It has often been reported that the eyes and mouths of people beheaded show signs of movement. It has been calculated that the human brain has enough oxygen stored for metabolism to persist for about seven seconds after the supply is cut off.

Various experiments have been made on guillotined heads and generally seem to show that very little consciousness remains after two to five seconds although some have concluded that the head retains feeling for much longer.

Andrew Allison, Tarporley, Cheshire

I have never heard of any victim coming back to tell us. Maybe your correspondent could volunteer to be a guinea-pig — in the cause of science.

Peter Rushforth, Bradford, West Yorkshire

In addition to your last answer, while I was recovering from neurosurgery some years ago, a consultant neurologist and I researched for how long after death certain reflexes could be elicited.

On delving into the history of neurology, we found that during the 1789 French Revolution, after a head had been severed by the guillotine, a researcher would grab it from the basket, hold it by the hair and turning it face to face, would ask a simple question: "What is your name?" Not infrequently the lips made meaningful movements.

Dr George Duncan, Aberlour, Banffshire

Robert Wynkefield, who witnessed the execution of Mary, Queen of Scots, reported that "her lips stirreded up and down a quarter of an hour after her head was cut off".

Tom Jago, London SW6

Folklore has it that Marie Antoinette (1755–1793) blushed when her severed head was slapped, but this is unlikely.

Antoine Laurent Lavoisier (1743–1794), who is regarded as the founder of modern chemistry, and who was a brilliant experimenter, fell foul of the Revolutionary hierarchy. On May 8, 1794, together with 27 others, he was guillotined. He had stated that he would communicate by blinking following decapitation and was reported to have managed nine or ten blinks.

Alun Morgan, Tenby, Pembrokeshire

It was not Marie Antoinette, but Charlotte Corday, executed on July 17, 1793, for the murder of Jean-Paul Marat, who allegedly blushed after her severed head was slapped by the assistant executioner (who was subsequently imprisoned for his breach of scaffold etiquette).

A Dr Beaurieux reported, after attending the execution of a certain M Languille in 1905, that: "Immediately after decapitation, the eyelids and lips of the guillotined man worked in irregularly rhythmic contractions for about five or six seconds. I waited for several seconds. The spasmodic movements ceased. The face relaxed, the lids half closed on the eyeballs, leaving only the whites of the conjunctiva visible, exactly as in the dying whom we have occasion to see every day in the exercise of our profession or as in those just dead. It was then that I called in a strong, sharp voice: 'Languille!' I saw the eyelids slowly lift up with an even movement, quite distinct and normal, such as happens in everyday life with people awakened or torn from their thoughts.

"Next, Languille's eyes very definitely fixed themselves on mine and the pupils focused themselves. I was not, then, dealing with the sort of vague dull look without any expression that can be observed any day in dying people to whom one speaks. I was dealing with undeniably living eyes which were looking at me. After several seconds the eyelids closed again, slowly and evenly, and the head took on the same appearance as it had before I called out. It was at that point that I called out again and once more, without any spasm, the eyelids lifted slowly and undeniably living eyes fixed themselves on mine with perhaps even more penetration than the first time. Then there was a further closing of the eyelids but now less complete. I attempted the effect of a third call; there was no further movement and the eyes took on the glazed look they have in the dead . . . The whole thing had lasted twenty-five to thirty seconds."

Alec McBarnet, London N6

The correspondence on this topic lends credibility to Orderic Vitalis's account of the judicial killing of Earl Waltheof (May 31, 1076): "[H]e began to say aloud 'Our Father, which art in Heaven'. But when he reached the last sentence and said 'And lead us not into temptation', the executioner struck off the earl's head. Then the severed head was heard by all present to say in a clear voice, 'But deliver us from evil. Amen'."

Ann Williams, London E11

Your last correspondent says that after Earl Waltheof was beheaded on May 31, 1076, he was heard to say in a clear voice "But deliver us from evil. Amen". There are two problems here. First, the axe blade would have smashed the larynx which contains the vocal chords. Secondly, speech is produced by airflow through the vocal cords and the source of the airflow, the lungs, would have been several feet away.

William Garrett, Harrow, Middlesex

A severed head will still have the majority of its cranial nerves intact. Therefore, it can blush, blink, move eyes and tongue, open mouth and smale. It can also see, hear, feel and respond. The only thing it cannot do is make a sound, as there is no longer a connection to the lungs.

There are about ten seconds worth of oxygen remaining before unconsciousness occurs and doubtless those ten seconds must seem a lifetime.

Dr David Evan, Leicester

During the early 1970s, I worked for a butcher during college holidays and my duties included fetching meat from local abattoirs. I still remember the shock of my first visit to see a row of five or six severed cows' heads hanging on hooks — all of which were still twitching furiously.

I imagine nothing remotely resembling consciousness remained but it did suggest that there was some vestige of a connection between brain and muscles some 20 minutes or more after slaughter.

I am a vegetarian these days.

John Heather, Leamington Spa, Warwickshire

Correspondence on this subject has concentrated on the head. The body may similarly react to severance as well as the head — the proverbial "headless chicken" effect.

An example of this was the 9th Earl of Argyll, after his execution in 1685. As his head fell, his body, in a macabre spasm, is said to have jumped upright on its feet, spouting blood "like a cascade or *jette d'eau*" (as a contemporary observed), before being pulled down by the executioner.

Professor Emeritus David Stevenson, University of St Andrews

Perhaps it might be a good idea to conclude on a lighter note with

Pooh Bah's explanation to the Mikado of Nanki Poo's supposed execution:

> Now though you'd have said the head was dead
> (For its owner dead was he)
> It stood on its neck, with a smile well bred
> And bowed three times to me!
> It was none of your impudent off-hand nods
> But as humble as could be
> For it clearly knew
> The deference due
> To a man of pedigree.

H. G. Hands, Reading

5. THIS SPORTING LIFE

When William Webb Ellis ran with the ball, why didn't the referee just blow his whistle for a foul?

Martin Bullock, Luton

No foul was called simply because there would have been no referee. Games at public schools in the early and mid-19th century were almost entirely self-policed. The assumption was made that if a gentleman inadvertently infringed the rules, he would take it upon himself to ensure that his team did not benefit from the breach.

This was taken to the extreme by the Corinthians association football team who, in the years after penalties were introduced to the game, refused to accpt them. If a penality was awarded against the Corinthians by a referee, the goalkeeper would merely stand by a post until the kick was taken, allowing the other team an easy goal.

Tom Rutherford, Edinburgh

The alleged incident took place in 1823. When boys played football at Rugby School at that time they did so without the assistance of a referee. The boys met before the game to agree the rules by which they were to play. This resulted in variations nearly every time they played. The boys wrote the rules in a series of exercise books, which can still be seen at the school. As anyone who has worked with children will verify, when children make up the rules of any game themselves they will obey those rules implicitly. The boys at Rugby School were no exception. Even in 1871, when the Rugby Football Union (RFU) was formed, the game was played 20 a side but still no referee.

There is very little evidence to support the assertion that William Webb Ellis was the first person to pick up the ball and run with it. In 1876 Martin Bloxam, who had left Rugby in 1820, wrote an account for the school magazine based on hearsay. This was immediately contested by a peer of Webb Ellis from his schooldays.

In 1895 the Old Rugbeians of the RFU set up a committee to try to keep the game in their control. They accepted the hearsay rather than a contemporary account. The journalist J. L. Manning investigated the investigators and concluded that the story was a perfect hoax and that the Old Rugbeians had falsified the history of rugby. By this time Webb

Ellis himself was dead and unable to confirm or deny the story. Several witnesses, including Thomas Hughes, of *Tom Brown's Schooldays* fame, contested the Webb Ellis story but their account was left out of the report. The committee completed the hoax by having the commemorative stone cut and placed in the headmaster's garden.

Thomas Hughes states that to run with the ball was considered extraordinary and even suicidal. If a boy did pick up the ball and run with it in 1823 it was either an accepted part of the game or a very foolish act, after the boys had met, agreed and written down the rules by which the game was to be played. That boy would have been branded a cheat and would have received what is termed today as a "good shoeing".

Nick White, Suffolk and North Essex Rugby Union Referees Society,
Sudbury, Suffolk

Why are points in lawn tennis scored as they are, that is fifteen for the first, fifteen for the second, and ten for the third?

Mike Glover, Bath

Scoring in tennis was originally 15, 30, 45, Game. Game represented 60 points and the 45 became abbreviated to 40. The analogy is with the minute hand of a clock, each point advancing by 15 minutes. Lawn tennis developed from the indoor game of *jeu de paume* which had matured in France, a country where 60 rather than 100 was once the major unit. (Thus the language has no simple word for 70 but the compound *soixante-dix*.) When Walter Wingfield patented his rules for the new game in 1874 he proposed scoring as in rackets: 1, 2, 3, etc to 15. This was overruled by the adherents of the indoor game and when the first lawn tennis tournament was held at Wimbledon three years later the scoring was the same as it is today.

Richard Wingfield, Reading

Richard Wingfield's answer is only partially correct as that excludes the scoring of a "set". Originally the scoring for each player (or side, if doubles) was done by moving a marker round a circle by 15 degrees for each point won and a game was completed after reaching 60 degrees. Six such games made a set and the marker was then moved around a full circle to start the second set, etc. The first two points, 15 and 30, remain the same and, as Richard Wingfield mentions, 45 is shortened to 40 and 60 to "game". This does not explain the provisions of "deuce" which appears to have been added later on, however, without disturbing the basic scoring system around a circle of 360 degrees.

Shafi Ahmed, East Acton, London

Why is a "local derby" so called?

Antony Gilder, Cheltenham

The term originates from the horse race of the same name. That race, first run in 1780, was named after Edward Stanley, 12th Earl of Derby. It soon became established as the high point of the racing season as part of the meeting at Epsom in Surrey in early June. It became so important that other classic races were named after it, such as the Kentucky Derby.

Derby Day, the day of the race, became a hugely popular event, not just for the toffs but as a big day out for all Londoners, a public holiday in all but name. In 1906 George R. Sims wrote: "With the arrival of Derby Day we have touched the greatest day of all in London; it may almost be said to be the Londoners' greatest holiday — their outing or saturnalia". Around this time, the word moved into more general use to describe any highly popular and well-attended event. In particular, it came to be applied to a fixture between two local sides, first called a "local derby" and then abbreviated.

Jo Leadbitter, Croydon, Surrey

If one looks at the development of football, both soccer and rugby, the common precursor is "camp ball", a game played from Roman times through to about 1600. The game was played in a defined area eg. the camp square, and consisted of two teams "scrummaging" with a "ball" — perhaps a lump of wood or stone — with the object of carrying the "ball" across a goal line. "Camp ball" developed into "hurling", and its derivatives, with the introduction of "cudgels". Time was no longer of the essence, and games could spread over hours if not days. The pitch was no longer defined and "goal lines" could be miles apart.

The most famous of these was between the Derby parishes of St Peter's and All Saints — from which the term "local derby" derives.

John Drapkin, Nottingham

Why were most English football teams simply named after their

location, while so many Scottish teams ignored geographical considerations and called themselves by such romantic appellations as St Johnstone (Perth), Queen of the South (Dumfries) or Heart of Midlothian (Edinburgh). South of the border, I think only Port Vale (Burslem) bucks this trend.

George Jenkins, Manchester

The question is quite right in that calling a football club Queen of the South is romantic. However, the title is ascribed to the town of Dumfries itself. In regards to St Johnstone Football Club, St Johntoun was the old name for the city of Perth.

In Edinburgh, under the tower of St Giles Cathedral on the Royal Mile (High Street), was a tolbooth which was demolished in 1817. The jail was known locally as the "Heart of Midlothian" and its site today is marked by a heart-shaped formation of causeway stones. In the early 1870s a dance club called Heart of Midlothian after the old tolbooth was established. A group of lads who frequented the dance club decided to form a football team and used the dance hall's name.

The football team Greenock Morton take part of their name from Morton Terrace, where some of their members lived. As for that famous remark "they'll be dancing in the streets of Raith tonight", the football club from Kircaldy take their name from the Laird of Raith because one of their football grounds was leased from him.

Kenny Gilchrist, Dalkeith, Midlothian

It is worth noting that during the initial period of Port Vale's career in the Football League (1892–1907), the name of the club was "Burslem Port Vale", reflecting the geographical fact that the club hailed from the North Staffordshire town of Burslem (the "mother town" of the Potteries towns), and was formed following a meeting at "Port Vale House" in that town. This town of Burslem later joined with five other towns to form the County Borough of Stoke-on-Trent (later City of Stoke-on-Trent). The prefix "Burslem" was dropped from the Port Vale name when the club moved to a new ground in the nearby town of Hanley in about 1911.

Another English club without geographical basis for its name is the North London Club "Arsenal". The name came originally from the South London club "Woolwich Arsenal".

David Gater, Hadlow, Kent

Why is Portsmouth also known as "Pompey"?

Dianne Woodham, Camberley, Surrey

It isn't. Portsmouth FC is known as Pompey but the city, as any Portmuthian will tell you, is either "Portsmouth" or "the City". "Pompey" (for the city) is the usage of visiting sailors, northern holidaymakers and business reps.

Michael Brown, Highbridge, Somerset

The nickname for the town comes from Portsmouth Football Club, which was originally a Royal Artillery team. In the 1898 Queen's Birthday Review, the Royal Artillery in Portsmouth were relegated to the role of lining the parade route rather than marching past. At the time, the French were held up to some ridicule by the British for lining parade routes in Paris with *les pompiers*, firemen in over-flamboyant uniforms with highly polished brass helmets. The Royal Navy matelots took the opportunity for some inter-Service ribbing by calling the gunners "Pompeys".

This became the nickname of the Royal Artillery football team and has been the affectionate title of Portsmouth Football Club for its fans ever since.

Russell Vallance, Royal Artillery Museum, London SE18

Why are football games between Celtic and Rangers known as "Old Firm" derbies?

Tom La Touche, London EC3

According to the co-authors Tom Campbell and Pat Woods in their book *A Celtic A-Z* (1992), the term "Old Firm" came into use in the early 20th century when the clubs' domination of Scottish football began. It referred to both the frequency of their meetings and the commercial spin-offs that resulted from this rivalry, and it was "half-admiring and half-critical". Apparently, cartoons of the time would depict officials of both clubs carrying bulging moneybags to the bank.

In the early 1980s, matches between the then dominant forces of Aberdeen and Dundee United became known as "New Firm" derbies, a term which has become pretty much redundant owing to the resurgence of the "Old Firm".

Brian Murray, Perth

Was football hooliganism in Britain completely unknown before the 1960s?

Graham Miller, Newcastle-upon-Tyne

In 1909, a Celtic v Rangers matched ended with the goalposts alight, barricades ablaze and more than a hundred people injured. Before that, in the last years of the 19th century, Arsenal, Sheffield Wednesday, Crewe Alexandra and Lincoln City were among clubs temporarily closed because of crowd disorder.

Earlier still, football was widely regarded as a violent pastime — "a friendlie kind of fight", to quote one 18th-century source.

Michael McManus, Leeds

The Black Country's premier team, West Bromwich Albion, and their Birmingham rivals, Aston Villa, are separated by a mere three miles. They have been adversaries for well over a century, and met for the first time in the second round of the Staffordshire Cup on December 9, 1882.

It is recorded that as the Albion team, accompanied by 3,000 supporters, made their way by wagon to the Villa ground, then situated in Perry Bar, "they had to run a gauntlet of stones and clods of earth hurled at them by rival supporters".

Albion drew the game 3–3, won the replay 1–0 and went on to lift their first trophy by beating Stoke 3–2 in the final in the Potteries.

David Watkin, Kingswinford, Staffordshire

On July 10, 1610, a gang of Border Scotsmen came to "the Ball-Green of the lands of Campbell" to play with "a wood futeball". Douglas of Drumlanrig complained that they "swaggered around with hagbuts and pistollets" and "in a bragging manner, barracked Douglas in his own den", making "provocation".

As a law-abiding descendant of one of this unruly mob, I am relieved to know that they were pardoned.

Paul Moynagh, Kingswear, Devon

Philip Stubbes (1543–93) wrote in the *Anatomie of Abuses in the Realme of England*: "Football causeth fighting, brawling, contention, quarrel-picking, murder, homicide, and a great effusion of blood, as daily experiences teaches."

Eddy Coulson, Harrow, Middlesex

When Scotland play the Republic of Ireland at football, which side do Celtic fans support?

Michael Dowsett, Kidlington, Oxfordshire

Among my friends who are Celtic fans, are some who keenly support Scotland, and others who support the Irish national team.

The key defining factor is whether they believe they are Scots, or Irishmen who live in Scotland.

Alistair Smith, London SW16

Speaking as a Celtic season-ticket and shareholder, I hope most fair-minded Celtic fans would support the team with the best chance of progressing to the finals of whatever World Cup or European Championship the two sides were playing in.

However, given identical circumstances, the majority of Celtic fans would give their support to the Republic of Ireland team for the following reasons:

A significant proportion of Celtic fans are Irish by birth; a far greater number can claim to be Irish by blood.

Because of past perceived discrimination against Celtic players by the SFA establishment. For instance, why did the wing legend Jimmy Johnstone receive so few Scottish caps at the expense of an inferior Rangers player?

More recent incidents of Celtic or former Celtic players being booed by "Scottish fans" while playing for their team (such as Brian McClair while he was at his peak with Manchester United).

The sectarian abuse suffered by Celtic players at the hands of "Northern Irish fans" while playing for their team (such as Neil Lennon).

As a result, most Celtic fans feel more culturally aligned with "Republican Ireland" than they do with "Unionist Scotland".

Paul Marron, Rushmere St Andrew, Suffolk

The confusion as to where their loyalty lies stems from the fact that many Irish people also support Celtic.

The one team that all their supporters would never support — against anyone — is England.

Gary Clark, Radlett, Hertfordshire

Having followed this discussion with interest, I am reminded of the saying that in Glasgow an atheist is someone who goes to a Celtic v Rangers match to enjoy the football.

Ian Proud, London W5

I understand that Middlesbrough were, until last weekend, the most successful football club in the country never to have won anything of significance. Which team now has this distinction?
John Mohan, Letchworth, Hertfordshire

Although this question is a bit of a contradiction in terms, as success in football is almost always measured in trophies, the current most high-profile club in England and Wales never to have won at least one major trophy is Fulham, which are at present ninth place in the Premiership.

Founded in 1879, Fulham have as their only claims to fame being FA Cup runners-up in 1975 and winning the Intertoto Cup in 2002. If one wishes to be generous to Fulham and allow them the Intertoto, then the next most successful trophyless club is Wigan Athletic, currently lying third in the Nationwide League First Division, which at least can claim two Associate Members Cup triumphs in the form of the Freight Rover Trophy in 1985 and the Auto Windscreens Shield in 1999.

Of the 92 Premiership and Football League clubs, no fewer than 44 have won at least one major trophy. Easily the all-time record holders are Liverpool with 41. Of the so-called "Big Three" at present, Manchester United have won 31, Arsenal 25 and Chelsea just the 9. Other big winners over the years have been Aston Villa (22), Spurs (16) and Everton (15). Fifteen clubs have won just one trophy.

Patrick Coffey, Heathfield, East Sussex

Birmingham City have a decent long-term record in this respect. They were the first English club to enter a European competition (Inter Cities Fairs Cup in May 1956), have spent this season in the top half of the Premiership and even made a profit in their last financial year — yet they have never won anything of significance, apart from the League Cup way back in wintry 1963.

Interestingly, Birmingham's manager, Steve Bruce, has made it clear that he attaches more importance to wins in the league rather than cup competitions, so perhaps Birmingham will retain this distinction until they win the Premiership.

Birmingham's closest contender for top underachievers is, your previous correspondent argues, Fulham. But for my money Birmingham just shade it because of their better longer-term record; as recently as 1996 Fulham stood in 91st position in the league so they cannot really be called "successful".

John Scrivens, Ruislip, Middlesex

Though your last correspondent makes a compelling case for Birmingham City — as opposed to Fulham — being the most successful football club in the country never (or hardly) to have won anything of significance, I would like to nominate Charlton Athletic.

Charlton's historical league profile is similar to that of Birmingham's. However, on a point of technicality, Charlton's 1947 FA Cup triumph precedes Birmingham's League Cup victory by 16 years. As neither club has won anything of significance since and both enjoy relative Premiership comfort, I would submit that these clubs share parity in respect of (un)achievement. Charlton may be viewed as slightly more "successful" as they returned (again) to the top division in 2000, while Birmingham only did so two years ago.

Michael Sheard, University of Teesside, Middlesbrough

Why do athletes run, walk and hurdle in an anti-clockwise direction when taking part in track events? Are there any exceptions?

Jennifer E. Goulding, Solihull, West Midlands

From 1984 to 1994 I was the technical director of the International Amateur Athletic Federation. During that time I received several letters asking this very question. Not knowing the answer myself, I contacted many of the world's leading athletics historians, statisticians, coaches and administrators. Not one knew the answer!

Several interesting theories were expounded, including: "Most athletes are right-footed (legged) and, therefore, prefer to push harder from the right, ie, when running anti-clockwise"; "with the heart being on the left of the body, the centre of gravity of the torso is to the left, thus favouring an anti clockwise motion"; even "the first Oxford v Cambridge race was held that way"!

There are no exceptions. However, in the discipline of race walking, there are several long distance track events such as 24-hour and six-day day races. In these, the athletes start off in an anti-clockwise direction but every hour they have to change direction and run anti-clockwise lest they get giddy.

Mike Gee, London SW18

Although I'm not certain about the reason for running anti-clockwise on running tracks (the Oxbridge reason is well quoted), may I suggest that in ultra-distance events such as 24 hours and 48 hours the reason for changing direction every three or four hours is not to prevent dizziness of the athletes but to ensure that they do not suffer any ill-effects to their muscles by going constantly around the same small circuit in the same direction. A bit like typists and such having RSI.

Dave Walsh, UKA Ultra Distance Team Manager,
West Wickham, Kent

In the pioneering days of track athletics in the 19th century, there was no conformity. Races were frequently run in a clockwise direction. The earliest tracks could be one third of a mile in length or more and were not always sited on level ground. The direction of running was arranged to give competitors as fair a run as possible. For example, a quarter-mile race would be around the most level and favourable section of the track and this might be in either direction. Some of the early AAA Championships and Olympic Games were run clockwise. It was not until the 1908 Olympics in London that the practice of anti-clockwise running was fully established.

However, those bastions of tradition, Oxford and Cambridge, continued to run clockwise at Iffley Road and Fenner's until after the Second World War, when their new quarter-mile tracks were built.

The rules for competition have it as a recommendation, not a law, that races be run left-hand inside, so it is still open to meeting organisers to buck the trend.

Peter Lovesey, Chichester

Athletics meetings were held at Stamford Bridge both before and after it became the home of Chelsea Football Club. A history of the stadium, *The Bridge* by Colin Benson, includes two photographs of races being run clockwise at the AAA Championships in 1898.

Anti-clockwise racing in sports stadiums is not confined to

athletics. Track cyclists, ice speed skaters, speedway riders and greyhounds all follow the same practice.

Brian Sharp, Ruislip, Middlesex

The Greeks always turned left-handed round the turning point — ie, anti-clockwise — in running distances more than one length of the stadium (eg, the *diaulos* and the *dolichos*). This practice is illustrated on a Panathenaic amphora of the 6th century BC. The Greeks also adopted the left-hand, anti-clockwise turn in chariot racing.

Michael Pope, Salisbury

Where were the planned venues for the Olympic Games of 1916, 1940 and 1944?

John Smith, Sunderland

The 1916 Games were allocated to Berlin, yet the Great War clearly made their being held impossible. The 1940 Games, despite the conflict between Japan and China, were given to Tokyo in 1936. However, owing to the escalation of the conflict, they were abandoned in 1938. Helsinki, which had registered the next highest vote in 1936, was offered the Games and accepted.

Despite the outbreak of the European war in 1939, plans went ahead. They were suspended during the period of the Winter War between Russia and Finland, which ended in March 1940. It soon became apparent that it would be impossible to go ahead as the war in the West intensified.

The 1944 Games, allocated to London, were a source of continuous communication between the International Olympic Committee and the British Olympic Association, before being abandoned in 1943.

Leslie Crouch, Cardiff

The Indian cricket team includes non-Hindus and, so far as I can remember, always has done. Has the Pakistani cricket team ever included non-Muslims?

Robert Jeffcoate, Bodfari, Denbighshire

I can count at least five non-Muslim cricket players who have represented Pakistan cricket at the highest level. Duncan Sharpe (a stylish batsman) and Antao D'Souza played for Pakistan in the late

1950s and early 1960s; both were Christians. Anil Dilpat (Hindu) was the wicket keeper in the days of Imran Khan (when Syed Kirmani, a Muslim, was India's wicket keeper) and now Yousuf Youhanna (Christian) and Danish Kaneria (Hindu) are members of Pakistan cricket team. Yousuf is of course a top quality batsman and Danish replaced Mushtaq Ahmad as a leg spinner in the team.

It is important to point out that more than 97 per cent of the Pakistan population is Muslim, whereas in India Muslims constitute almost 15 per cent of the population — hence the relatively greater representation of Muslims in the Indian cricket team

Dr S. Ijzaal H. Zaidi, Rotherham, South Yorkshire

Has a cricket side in an international match — or any other first class match — ever reached or exceeded an innings score of 1,000?

Michael Knight, Geneva

This has never happened in Tests and only twice in first-class cricket. Both instances were in Australia in the 1920s.

In February 1923, Victoria played a much weaker Tasmania and scored 1,059. Playing in only his third match, Victoria's captain Bill Ponsford hit 429 to set a new world record for a batsman. Victoria won by an innings and 666 runs. Over the Christmas holiday of 1926, Victoria scored 1,107 against New South Wales. Ponsford was one of only two of the batsmen left from the earlier side. This time he hit a more modest 352 while his colleague Jack Ryder scored 295. This time Victoria won by an innings and 656.

The next highest score in all cricket was in a Test in August 1997, when Sri Lanka batted on and on after starting the final day 50 ahead of India's 537 for eight. Sri Lanka's Sanath Jayasuriya was on 326 and everyone hoped he would beat Brian Lara's Test record of 375. In fact Jayasuriya was out for 340 but Sri Lanka continued to end the match on 952 for six. The whole thing was a pointless draw.

Michael Baws, Little Hereford

6. THAT'S ENTERTAINMENT

Did primitive man have a sense of humour? When and what was the first recorded joke?

Paul de la Sautée, London W1

It must be Adam's palindromic introduction to Eve "Madam, I'm Adam".

Archie Thomson, Whitby, North Yorkshire

My wife suggests, rather unkindly, "And God created Man".

David Dean, Manchester

The first recorded joke comes from a Sumerian text of 2000 BC, and was played out as a kind of improvised game between two wits. It went something to the effect of:

"The good news is that I have a good harvest."

"But the bad news is that you have no labourers to harvest it."

"The good news is that my neighbour says I can borrow his labourers."

"But the bad news is that your neighbour has already promised them to someone else."

"The good news is that the other harvest is very small and won't take them long."

"But the bad news is that while they are harvesting the other one, your harvest is attacked by a plague of locusts."

"The good news is that the locusts are all drowned in a thunderstorm."

"But the bad news was that this also flattens your harvest . . ."

The joke goes on, getting ever more outlandish, until one player capitulates.

Francis Kinsman, Bath

It is well known that Bertie Wooster was frequently engaged to be married, and always managed to escape matrimony, with Jeeves's help. But was he ever genuinely in love with any woman, rather than just briefly infatuated or proposing for lack of anything else to do?

Chris Campling, Sudbury, Suffolk

I quote from the master. "She resembled a particularly goodlooking schoolboy who had dressed up in his sister's clothes." This is Bobby Wickham who has been pretty extensively wooed for years, with no business resulting. Bertie is twice engaged to her, and is perennially attracted by her. Jeeves, as always, prevents any permanent alliance. The lady appears in four volumes of the saga and is the archetype of the female hell-raisers Wodehouse depicted so superbly.

Bob Ellis, Southport, Lancashire

Tricky question this, which even Jeeves might have had difficulty answering. Cora (Corky) Potter-Pirbright did seem to be a candidate, and, as your previous correspondent said, possibly Bobby Wickham. Pauline Stoker was the only woman found in his bed (admittedly when he was not there). I rather feel that his favourite was Aunt Dahlia, beside whom any other competition might pale. Of course, consummation would be beyond the pale. (Besides, she hadn't had her ankle tickled since the York and Ainsty Hunt Ball in 1921.)

Mark Powlson, Ashtead, Surrey

Bertie Wooster had two childhood sweethearts and six young ladies to whom he was superficially attracted but did little or nothing about pursuing. There were two girls (Vanessa Cook and Cynthia Wickhammersley) to whom he proposed quite deliberately and genuinely, but by whom he was rejected. There were eight others to whom he was engaged, in a total of 16 separate engagements, who were certainly not persons with whom he was in love in reality, the only voluntary engagement among them being the first of his four to Florence Craye, when he had been over-influenced by her wonderful profile.

The one girl to whom he proposed for the right reasons, and by whom he was accepted for the right reasons, was the American, Pauline Stoker. Their engagement was broken off by her father and although Bertie subsequently seemed to accept that this had been for the best, she was the one fiancée whom the reader has a sneaking suspicion he really would like to have married.

Tony Ring, Great Missenden, Buckinghamshire

Jeeves was not always responsible for the failure of Wooster's romances to become permanent alliances. The engagement to Pauline Stoker was broken off at her father's insistence because of the accounts of Bertie's behaviour that had been given by Sir Roderick Glossop, the

psychiatrist. He had concluded that Bertie was "barmy to the core".
Michael Ryan, Swansea

There was Lady Florence Craye, the first of the women Jeeves disapproved of. Bertie fancied himself in love with her, before "Types of Ethical Theory" put him off. Roberta ("Bobbie") Wickham, the red-haired Jezebel, as your previous correspondents said, was another candidate. The hot water bottle episode combined with Sir Roderick's Glossop's wrath and proof of her treachery causes Bertie to fall out of love as quickly as he fell in.

Then there was Gwladys Somebody. Gwladys, an artist, portrays Bertie with a kind of hungry, slavering look — fit material for the Slingby's Superb Soup ads. Bertie doesn't really fall out of love with Gwladys, but it's expedient that he leaves town. When he returns, he's confronted not only by the ads, but also by the news that Gwladys is now engaged to Lucius Pym.
Rashmi Rao, Bangalore

Bertie Wooster did marry Bobby Wickham — at least in C. Northcote Parkinson's imaginative "biography", *Jeeves, A Gentleman's Gentleman* (1979).
Alan Day, Sandbach, Cheshire

"Doh, ray, me, fah" etc for the musical scale. Why?
Les Deakin, Warrington, Cheshire [11/07/02]

The Tonic Solfa is based on the system devised, or possibly perfected, by Guido D'Arezzo, a Benedictine monk from France (*c*.995–1050). He was a musical theoretician and expanded the existing two lines of musical annotation to four lines. His system was based on a hexachord of six consecutive notes spaced by four tones and one semi-tone, mi-fa. In order to teach sight-reading to choirboys, he named the notes according to the syllables sung at that note in a hymn to St John composed by Paulus Diaconus. The original scale was Ut, Re, Mi, Fa, Sol, La.

Ut queant laxis, Resonare fibris,
Mira gestorum, Famuli tuorum,
Solve pollutis, Labiis reatum,
Sancte Iohannes.

By singing the hymn, a pupil could learn to recognise and reproduce each of the notes. Si was later added (Sancti Iohannes). Ut was eventually replaced by Doh (Domini, perhaps), it being considered easier to sing — probably in the 16th century. Si was replaced by Te in England in the 19th century, although Si is still used in many countries.

Brigadier Bill Bewley, Stranraer, Dumfries and Galloway

Did Henry VIII really write *Greensleeves*? If so, did he write anything else?

Cliff Skudder, Letchworth, Hertfordshire

On my frequent schools visits I have to correct this popular myth. The version we all know first appeared in 1584, in a book of ballads called *A Handefull of Pleasant Delites*. The earliest reference to *Greensleeves* is in the Stationers' Register in 1580. By this time Henry VIII had been dead for 33 years.

He did, however, compose music and write many other songs. His life as a young prince was designated to the Church and part of his training was in music. He wrote masses, motets and anthems in Latin. As King he continued to compose, adopting the recorder as his favourite instrument. His more popular songs are *Time to pass with goodly sport, Pastime with good company* and *Whereto should I express?*

Dante Ferrara, Lincoln

There are left-handed guitars but has anyone ever created a left-handed piano?

George Patterson, Durham

In Paris in 1878, following a proposal by the pianist Jozef Wieniawski, Edouard and Alfred Mangeot built several two-manual pianos in which the upper manual was reversed. One of these can be seen in the Musical Instrument Museum in Brussels.

Hugh Davies, London N4

In September 1997 I commissioned the first ever complete, left-handed piano. It was built by Poletti & Tuinman Fortepiano Makers in Utrecht and completed in July 1998. It is a mirror image of a 19th-century piano; the high notes begin on the left and the low notes on the right.

The pedals are reversed and the lid opens from the opposite side. As I am a left-handed concert pianist, it allows my dominant hand to take more of the elaborate and melodic lines. I am still able to play in the conventional way, but, despite years of training, I find it more instinctive to play in reverse.

The piano was first exhibited at the Bruges International Music Festival in 1998 and I gave the world premiere performance at the Queen Elizabeth Hall, London in 1999.

The next concert takes place at Bishopsgate Hall on April 1 (not an April fool!).

Christopher Seed, Twyford, Hampshire

Dublin lays claim to being the venue for the first performance of Handel's *Messiah* on April 13, 1742. However, I have heard that Handel first conducted a performance in Chester, while on his way to Holyhead and thence Dublin. Is there any evidence to back this claim?

Roy Jenkinson, Exmouth, Devon

Dublin was indeed the venue for the first public perfomance of *Messiah*, but during the second week of November 1741, en route to Dublin, Handel found himself stranded in Chester awaiting a favourable wind. Impatient to try out some of the *Messiah* choruses, he enlisted the help of local choristers from the cathedral to rehearse the music at his lodgings, the Golden Falcon Inn in Northgate Street.

Handel was not pleased with the result, for after many attempts the lead chorister was unable to sing the chorus *And with his stripes we are healed*. Handel lost his temper, swore in four or five languages, and cried out in broken English: "You scoundrel! Did you not tell me you could sing at sight?" The chorister replied: "Yes, sir, and so I can, but not at first sight."

David Willoughby, Barnet, Hertfordshire

When we face the music, what piece of music is being played?
Bill Coles, Edinburgh

My father used to describe "facing the music" as the aural onslaught he met each evening on returning from work, as the stereos of us three children competed to drown out the other's "rubbish".

Conversely, we children considered *Songs of Praise* a cruel form of retaliation.

Steve Williams, Epsom, Surrey

The phrase originates from the practice of the congregation turning to face the musicians in church. The memoirs of the Rev J. E. Linnell (1843–1919) give an account of the church services in the 1850s in his native Silverstone. I quote from *Old Oak*, originally published in 1932:

"I can just remember the band; it consisted of two copper key-bugles, two trombones, two clarionets, a two-valved cornopean, a shanked trumpet, a piccolo, a flute, a fiddle or two, and a venerable-looking bass viol. It sat with the choir up in the west gallery and, when Joseph from his cabin, announced: 'We will now sing to the praaise an' gloory o' God hymn number so-and-so,' all the congregation made a right-about turn and faced them."

The church has been rebuilt since then and no longer contains a west gallery. Alas the band is no more, and the lively choir is no longer at the west end of the church.

Gareth Salisbury, Towcester, Northamptonshire

It is not uncommon to hear an explanation of "facing the music" as deriving from the days when a church band and choir were in the west gallery. This always seems unconvincing in that it bears no relation to the accepted usage of the phrase, as in standing boldly before an impending threat.

One thinks rather of the drums and pipes of enemy troops marching out of the mist towards your lines.

R. G. Hodgson, Crowborough, East Sussex

The orchestral conductor faces the audience at the start of the concert to acknowledge their applause of greeting. He then turns 180 degrees and faces the music in both the music score before him and the orchestra performing. From that point on all is up to him; he alone is ultimately responsible for the performance and cannot evade that duty. He is "facing the music".

C. Y. Nutt, Cambridge

Whenever I see television programmes on life in other countries such as Ireland, Scotland, Wales, Austria, France, Italy, Spain and

Greece, I am inspired by the instantly recognisable background music used to portray the personality of each country. Which pieces of music do programme makers from around the world tend to use to impart the "sound" of England?

Richard Brown, Poole, Dorset

Stopping recently in the town square of Murat, a small resort in the Auvergne, France, I heard an open-air concert by local musicians devoted to music representing other European countries. A local school orchestra played the *Blue Danube* to represent Austria, and a male voice choir sang the *Volga Boatmen* for Russia.

I naturally waited for England's turn, and was rewarded by a brass band playing *Roll Out the Barrel*.

Will Werry, Cheltenham

Three years ago I was taken to see and hear a wonderful performance of "Musical Fountains" in Singapore which featured the flags of various nations together with appropriate music. We wondered what could be used for England and were delighted with *In an English Country Garden*.

Guy Chapman, Salisbury

Whenever an English ski party entered the only nightclub in Andermatt, Switzerland, in the late-1950s, the band always struck up a rendition of *It's a Long Way to Tipperary*.

David Morris-Marsham, London SW12

Who wrote the first piece of classical music?

Malcolm Kinnear, Briston, Norfolk

The word "classical" is not really susceptible of definition, especially when you remember that Classic FM would lump Gershwin, Adiemus and music for any film in the "classical" category. Moreover, in the 21st century there is a tendency to assimilate into the classical canon music — such as that of the trouvères — that would not then have had the kind of intellectual status that we now ascribe to what we term serious or "classical" music. But "wrote" may be the operative word here. If you accept Ambrosian and Gregorian chant into the category of classical music, then the first person to write it down would almost certainly have been an anonymous scribe in a monastery. Hildegard of Bingen may lay claim to being the first named composer that we know of.

On the other hand, if you mean classical as opposed to Baroque or Romantic (ie, from about 1760 until middle-period Beethoven), then Johann Christian Bach is as good a candidate as any.

Nigel Forde, York

Why are so many jazz musicians called "Art"? I can straightaway think of at least 15, but very few in other musical genres.

Barry Daniels, Bradford, West Yorkshire

The early generations of jazz musicians came disproportionately from the small American black middle class. Most were boys with classical musical training, paid for by parents who were usually aspirational professionals. Such aspirations find their way into the names we give, and in America in the first half of the 20th century "Arthur" was a markedly middle-class name with English (hence posh) connotations.

However, jazz developed its own mythology as a music that had come not from well-off urban centres (as it had in fact done), but rural roadhouses and working-class juke joints. This mythology, largely the work of white journalists, contributed to the appeal of jazz as a supposedly "primitive", hence earthy music, but it did not sit well with names like Percy and Arthur.

The monosyllabic "Art" had the right sound, though, and once established as a jazz name by giants like Art Tatum, it took on its own momentum as the obvious nickname for all those Arthurs whose mothers had dreamed of Camelot, but who themselves opted to ditch Bach for Be-bop.

J. E. Joseph, Edinburgh

How do the people who booed and shouted "Judas" at Bob Dylan in 1966 feel about him now?

Andy Neal, Chichester, West Sussex

It would be nice to think they have come to their senses. The two claimants — sadly now deceased — to be the voice of "Judas" recorded in that peerless 1966 concert in Manchester both came to feel their attitude foolish. C. P. Lee explains (see his article in the *Isis Bob Dylan*

Anthology published by Helter Skelter) how the booing and walkouts were orchestrated by the Singers Clubs with their "Stalinistic policy rules" — with original links to the Communist Party of Great Britain. Ewan MacColl said in 1987 that he had been opposed to us "becoming an arm of American cultural imperialism . . . That's the way I saw it as a political thinker at the time, and that's the way I still see it", so he never changed his petty-minded opposition to Bob Dylan.

C. P. Lee concludes that "the protesters [at the 1966 Dylan concerts] were not the majority, but they were certainly the most vocal". My colleague Bryan was at the Manchester concert and he remembers hearing a shout not of "Judas" but "Bob Dylan — the greatest living poet since Dylan Thomas", a not entirely coherent understatement, but eminently more sensible.

Jim Heppell, Lincoln

The fan who shouted "Judas" was Keith Butler. Keith, with whom I shared accommodation when we were both undergraduates at Keele University in the mid-1960s, emigrated to Canada many years ago. Sadly, he died last year, from cancer, I believe. As far as I know, although he may eventually have become reconciled to the "electrified Bob Dylan" as he used to call him, he always preferred the acoustic Dylan of the early 1960s.

Malcolm Steven, Dunstable

Contrary to your last answer, my cousin, John Cordwell, was the authentic claimant to the voice of "Judas". This was verified by Andy Kershaw, who did a sound test and interview with John some years ago. Following John's sudden death in 2001, Andy paid tribute to him in a radio programme. John never lost his respect for Dylan and grew to accept him going electric.

Harry Wormleighton, Rochdale

In the film *Pulp Fiction*, what is in the briefcase?
Richard Marlow, Sevenoaks, Kent

Apparently, Quentin Tarantino originally envisaged that the briefcase contained diamonds from the robbery in *Reservoir Dogs*, but eventually it was left unspecified. It was felt that the audience's imagination would provide limitless possible solutions to this conundrum.

An urban myth has grown that the briefcase contained Marsellus Wallace's soul, perhaps justified by the large Elastoplast on the back of Wallace's neck, the site that Satan prefers to remove souls from. This theory could be further supported by the case's miraculous protection of both Jules and Vincent when shot at by the "hand cannon", and the fact that Tim Roth's character declares it "beautiful" when peering into the briefcase.

In fact, I understand the case contained little other than a couple of batteries and an orange light bulb . . .

Andy Simms, Dunnington, Warwickshire

Who was the first movie star?

John O'Byrne, Dublin

The first "movie star" to be known by name, and in her native Germany, was Henny Porten (1888–1960). The daughter of a former German opera singer, Porten was born in Magdeburg. Oskar Messter, reputedly the inventor of the close-up shot, first brought Porten's performances to the screen.

Up to 1910, producers, especially members of the Motion Picture Patents Company, deliberately refused to reveal the true identities of actors and actresses on the assumption that public familiarity would make them difficult to control and that they would demand ever-increasing fees. However, Carl Laemmle established Florence Lawrence (1886–1938) as the first American film star (she was, in fact, born in Canada) when he poached her away from the Biograph Company to work for him at IMP.

She had, until then, been known simply as the "Biograph Girl". Laemmle publicised her real name. He continued this practice for his other contract artistes, thus initiating the American star system.

The UK's first movie star was Gladys Sylvani (c.1885–1953). Her name appears in publicity for *Stolen Letters*, which had its premiere on December 24, 1911.

John Cabrera, Grayshott, Surrey

Laemmle created the first movie publicity stunt by starting rumours that Florence Lawrence had died in an accident, then having her suddenly reappear alive and well. She was paid $1,000 a week, given screen credit, and, in 1911, was interviewed by *Motion Picture Story*, considered to be the first movie star interview.

The first fan magazines appeared in 1911 and two stars soon eclipsed Florence Lawrence. Mary Pickford and Charlie Chaplin were the first stars to achieve international fame. By 1916 they were both earning $10,000 a week. They were the first movie stars to reach levels of fame and fortune that stars of today possess.

Joe Luchok, Arlington, Virginia

What is the origin of the term "spaghetti western"? All the westerns I have watched have nothing to do with Italy.

Louise Costello, London SW4

Between 1960 and 1975, European film production companies made nearly 600 westerns. Critics either blasted or ignored these films, and because most of them were financed by Italian companies, they called them spaghetti westerns. Fans of the genre embraced the term which is now lovingly used to label any western made and financed by continental filmmakers.

Paul Anderson, Loughborough

The term "spaghetti western" was applied to westerns made with Italian finance, directors, composers and mainly Italian actors in supporting roles and filmed in the wildest areas of Spain.

An American actor who was either on the way up (cheap to employ) or past his prime usually took the lead as a soldier of fortune, who was almost as vicious and lacking in moral scruples as the villains he shot.

The term "spaghetti western" was first coined by American critics of the Italian western and was intended as a derogatory description. Other culinary labels used to describe these westerns included "sauerkraut westerns" (produced in East Germany) and "paella westerns" (international co-productions shot in Spain).

Noel Sturt, Christchurch, Dorset

The original "spaghetti western" movie was *A Fistful of Dollars* (1964), which was directed by Sergio Leone (Italian), made a big-screen star of Clint Eastwood, and was shot on a shoestring budget in Spain, with a mainly European cast. This was followed in quite short order by *For a Few Dollars More* and *The Good, The Bad and The Ugly*.

These films are characterised by a hero who, in many ways, is no better than bad guys, as well as gritty performances, and are the anti-thesis of the Hollywood western, where the good guy always wins and rides off into the sunset with the girl. In the spaghetti western, the hero rides off into the sunset with a bag of gold.

J-P. S. Kamester, London W14

Why do the scriptwriters of soap operas feel it necessary to have their characters say "Woss goin' on?" so frequently?

Peter Hamilton, Walton on Thames, Surrey

The phrase "Woss goin' on?" is a device used by scriptwriters to enable the character thus addressed to push the storyline along. It is for precisely this reason "What are you doing here?" is used in virtually every episode of *The Archers*.

Pamela Rose, Cowes, Isle of Wight

If everybody you thought you respected was constantly trying to cover up sleeping with your mother by burning your business down; if your former business partner was extorting "fahsands of pahns" from you over a doomed love affair with a gay priest; if you were dying of everything; if no one ever, ever wanted to get happily married to you and just move to another area . . .

If no one ever watched or even commented on the football or cricket; if your best pals frequently bunked off work for the afternoon and then later asked you to hang on to an unlicensed firearm "for a while, 'til things cool down", and then fled to "Spayne" or "Saaf Africa" . . .

If every other child was abducted, or dead by five years old; if your new wife always left you just after the onset of a new business disaster; if every geezer that you knew spoke as if he had a throat complaint, and always bought his new Lexus with cash . . .

If every pub sold only "bottles of lager and whatever She's having"; if every local shopgirl was an anorexic nymphomaniac kleptomaniac with a guilty drugs mule secret; if every "fella" was "only human" for having murdered his cross-dressing step-brother for microwaving his entire whelk-farm . . .

What else would you do but go and kneel sobbing beneath the rain "dahn the square" bellowing: "Woss goin' on?!"

Nick Slater, Northampton

The most common equivalent in Hollywood productions — one to be heard in almost every old black-and-white mystery movie — is to have a character say "I don't understand", thus inviting an illumination of the plot.

John Cottrell, Addlestone, Surrey

Who is, or was, the world's most prolific author in terms of words written?

A. J. Roberts, Shoreham-by-Sea, West Sussex

One of the most prolific writers was Isaac Asimov, but for the sheer quantity of books written it's Georges Simenon, at more than 400. This Belgian author was the creator of the fictional detective Inspector Maigret and it was said that he had periods when he could write two or three novels a month.

Glenti Bajrami, London NW5

The Spaniard, Lope de Vega (1562–1635), penned more than 1,500 plays, while he also wrote poetry and novels. His miscellaneous writings were published in 21 volumes. In addition, he sailed with the Armada of 1588 and took holy orders in 1614.

Desmond Hartley, Windermere, Cumbria

Barbara Cartland wrote over 700 books — not a great literary icon perhaps but she amused me vastly when I was a teenager.

Maureen Robinson, Belfast

The ancient scholar Didymus of Alexandria (1st century BC) is credited with having written between three and four thousand books (of which a single papyrus, found in a rubbish heap, survives). Rhazes, polymathic Persian author of several hundred works, once recalled: "In a single year I have written as many as 20,000 pages in a script as minute as that used for amulets. I was engaged fifteen years upon my great compendium, working night and day, until my sight began to fail and the nerves of my hands were paralysed".

His contemporary, the Arab historian Tabari, is said to have written forty pages every day throughout his long life. Voltaire left behind 15 million words; his letters alone fill 100 volumes. Jean-Paul Sartre wrote up to 10,000 words a day. The bibliography of Bertrand Russell lists more than 3,000 published items and itself fills three volumes; he also wrote 40,000 letters. A. C. Benson, Master of Magdalene College, Cambridge, published 100 books and kept a diary of 5 million words, filling 180 manuscript volumes, enough to fill 40 volumes of print; after his death, whole shelf-fuls of unpublished books, stories, essays and poems were consigned to the flames.

Graham Chainey, Brighton

It has been estimated that Charles Hamilton, creator of Billy Bunter and author of the Greyfriars and other school stories, wrote 70 million words over a period of almost half a century, the equivalent of 1,000 full-length novels.

Patrick Morley, Shipham, Somerset

Fifty years ago I heard the inebriate's version of *Twinkle, twinkle, little star* which began "Starkle, starkle, little twink / Who the hell am I do you think?" In fifty years now I have never been able to remember the final two lines. Can anyone out there help?

Peter Jenkins, Nantwich, Cheshire

I believe that the original (which I recall seeing many years ago) may have been written by Brian Cavell, and reads:

Starkle, Starkle little twink
Who the hell you are I think
I'm not under what you call
The alcho-fluence of inco-hol
I'm just a little slort on sheep
I'm not drunk like thinkle peep
I don't know who me yet
But the drunker I stand here
The longer I get
Just give me one more drink to fill my cup
'Cause I got all day sober to Sunday up.

Alan Simmons, London N3

Further to your correspondent's theory, I believe the correct author of this rhyme is the Australian poet, C. J. Dennis (1876–1938), and it is taken from his "My Doreen" series.

Margaret Robinson, Yeovil, Somerset

This version was recited by my grandmother in the 1940s:

> Scintillate, scintillate globule vivific
> Fain would I fathom thy nature specific
> Loftily poised in ether capacious
> Strongly resembling a gem carbonaceous.

John Prince, East Molesey, Surrey

Following your original answer my daughter Rachel, aged three, delighted us recently with a modernised version of the childhood classic:

> Twinkle twinkle chocolate bar
> My Daddy drives a rusty car
> Start the engine
> Pull the choke
> Off we go in a cloud of smoke
> Twinkle twinkle chocolate bar
> My dad drives a rusty car.

C. A. Hall, Wadhurst, East Sussex

According to some commentators Charles Dodgson — Lewis Caroll — was a user of psilocybe mushrooms, otherwise known as "magic mushrooms". Hence, perhaps:

> Twinkle, twinkle little bat
> How I wonder what you're at
> Up above the world so high
> Like a tea-tray in the sky.

Michael Knight, Geneva

We learnt the following at school a long time ago in Glasgow:

> Twinkle, twinkle, little star
> How I wonder what you are
> A cloud of unexploded gas
> Condensing to a solid mass.

Nora Howland, Broadstairs, Kent

> Twinkle, twinkle, little star
> I don't wonder what you are
> For by spectroscopic ken
> I know you are hydrogen.

Professor A. J. Meadows, Seagrave, Leicestershire

Did the art of limerick writing ever enjoy a "golden age" and is it now dormant?

M. W. T. Bullock, Wickham Bishops, Essex

A doubting young fellow from Wickham
Thought limericks were down, so he'd kick 'em
    but his lines to *The Times*
    were blank verse, with no rhymes.
I propose that we tell him to stick 'em.

Bill Meehan, Great Totham, Essex

The limerick lives, it's not dormant
It goes on like my wife does — a torment;
    To think that it's dead
    Is to put in my head
All manner of thoughts that it oughtn't.

David Meredith, Aberystwyth

As I sought a good rhyme for "cormorant"
Mr Bullock asked "Lim'ricks dormorant?"
    He's nothing to fear –
    They're flourishing here
Sincerely, your millionth informorant.

Chris Walker, Emsworth, Hampshire

Since it is almost impossible to find a clean limerick, the golden age obviously began with the invention of the lavatory wall. It has continued until fairly recent times when it was found to be incompatible with the txt msg.

Cliff Skudder, Letchworth, Hertfordshire

The limerick form didn't die
You'll see it again bye-and-bye
    Clean and grammatical
    It's on a sabbatical
(And that's strictly between you and I!)

Moss Rich, Hove, East Sussex

7. THE WAY OF THE WORLD

The British have their own names for many European cities, so that Brunswick is Braunschweig, Florence is Firenze. Do Europeans have their own names for British cities?

Raymond Snell, Redditch, Worcestershire

Here in Italy, we have our own names for the capital cities, so that London and Edinburgh become Londra and Edimburgo. Also Dublin is known as Dublino, Paris is translated as Parigi, and Prague as Praga. All European cities other than the capitals retain their original names.

Elena Baldissera, Spinea, Venezia

Elena Baldissera errs when she says that in Italian all "European cities other than capitals retain their original names". In Italian Munich is Monaco (confusingly), Marseilles is Marsiglia, Lyons Lione, Hamburg Amburgo, Breslau Breslavia, Thebes Tebe and so on. Whether or not the foreign form is retained in Italian depends on historical usage. Towns or cities that had notable contact with Italy and Italians in the Middle Ages tended to develop Italianised names (eg, Parigi, Londra, Marsiglia, Monaco or Praga) whereas those medieval cities with fewer Italian ties (normally commercial) tended to pass into modern Italian with their original foreign names (eg, Oxford, Cambridge).

Robert Black, University of Leeds

The French certainly do. Witness Londres, Douvres, Edimbourg and Cantorbery. They extend this practice to Aix-la-Chapelle (Aachen), Cologne (Köln) and Cordoue (Córdoba). The Spanish have Argel (Algiers), Ginebra (Geneva) and Marsella (Marseille — or do I mean "Marseilles"?)

John Grisbrooke, Ware, Hertfordshire

The Welsh are certainly European, and they have Caer for Chester, Efrog for York, and Llundain for London.

Peter Pickering, London N12

My favourite one, even if not European, is the Indian speaker's "La.n.dan", which with its full-blown retroflex palatals, has a sonant richness which the English speaker's tongue cannot get round. My home city of Edinburgh, itself a curious mix of the Gaelic and the Germanic, has a different pronunciation and spelling for every major European language, not to mention some complex non-European offerings from the Chinese and the Japanese — "Ejinbara", no less.

Ian Astley, School of Asian Studies, University of Edinburgh

I recently mounted an expedition to the source of the River Thames near Cirencester. On reaching my destination, I found a large marker stone on the edge of a completely dry field, with no obvious direction for water to flow, even had there been any. Acknowledging the existence of several tributaries, where does the Thames actually rise?

Tony Doyle, Deanshanger, Northamptonshire

It is not surprising that your correspondent is bemused. Fred Thacker (*The Thames Highway*, 1914) recorded studying papers written in 1746 that indicated the rivalry between locations claiming to be the true source.

The River Thames oozes from the ground through the Cotswold Jurassic limestone in a number of places. The location of these springs has changed over the centuries as water abstraction from the underlying limestone and land usage has intensified. However, the three most commonly quoted locations for the actual source are at Trewsbury Mead, near the Thames Head pub; Lyd Well near Kemble; and Seven Springs, about 12 miles north of Cirencester.

Thames Head has the merit of being recognised as "The Source" by the Ordnance Survey, and is marked as such on all its maps. The Thames Commissioners and subsequently the Thames Conservancy recognised this location as the official source and placed a statue of the recumbent Old Father Thames here.

Lyd Well, about one mile downstream from Thames Head, can contribute a more obvious flow of water and has been a secure source of water over the years. The water rises in a muddy copse before joining the infant Thames about 30 paces away.

Seven Springs has had a number of proponents for its claim to be the true source (including the Romans). By casual observation, it certainly flows more consistently than the spring at Thames Head, it is the furthest distance you can travel upstream from the sea, and is at the highest level from which water flows over land into the River Thames. However, it is regarded by most people as being a tributary of the River Thames, and is called the River Churn.

My wife and I were fortunate to see the Thames Head spring gurgling forth in the early 1990s, but 12 months later, when we started the Thames Path walk, it was completely dry, but the slight depression through the adjacent pastures does indicate the presence of an occasional flow. There was a flow from Lyd Well, but this soon disappeared into the bed, and we did not see the stripling Thames as a recognisable entity until we reached Ewen.

Stuart Darby, Wallingford, Oxfordshire

Is there any old map anywhere that actually says "Here be dragons"?

Patrick Martin, Winchester, Hampshire

The phrase, although a good description of the ancient view of uncharted regions, does not appear on any ancient maps; it does appear by the Renaissance era. In this period, the cartographer's language was Latin, not English. The phrase "HC SVNT DRACONES" (*Hic sunt dracones*) appears on the East coast of Asia on the Lenox Globe (*c.* 1503–07). This globe is a 13cm copper globe bought in Paris in 1855, and now part of the New York Public Library.

There is a modern map which contains the English phrase. "Here There Be Dragons" was used for the unknown north polar region (labelled "Terra Incognita") of the asteroid Vesta in a paper by Michael Gaffey of Rensselaer Polytechnic, New York State, submitted to the planetary science journal *Icarus* (Vol. 128, No. 1, July 1997).

Will Smith, London SW15

The oldest map from Ancient Mesopotamia is written on a clay tablet; from Babylonia, it dates to around 700BC.

It shows in eclectic and schematic form a number of countries, cities and waterways. The accompanying text, alas badly damaged, lists the various animals in different outlying regions, including a region inhabited by "the viper, the great sea serpent, the Anzu-bird and the scorpion man". The map is on display at the British Musuem.

Dr John MacGinnis, McDonald Institute for Archaeological Research, Cambridge

Embellishment of blank areas of early maps with factoids is not new. The Peutinger Table — a 4th-century road map of the entire world known to its Roman cartographers — doesn't have, so far as I can see, "Here be dragons", but the further reaches of Persia and India, which are pretty sketchy, include mountain ranges with two warnings: "*In his locis scorpiones nascuntur*", and "*In his locis elephanti nascuntur*" — ie, here be scorpions and elephants.

The extreme south-east of the map simply says "*Piratae*".

Robin Birch, Oxford

All our maps and atlases show North to be "up". Why is this? Did any indigenous peoples in the southern hemisphere have South at the top, even in local maps and charts?

Tom Morley, Cuffley, Hertfordshire

North is at the top of a map because you can orientate it by pointing the top of it at the pole star Polaris. This is the only fixed point in the northern hemisphere, where maps were invented. Polaris's position in the sky is fixed because it happens to lie on the extension of the Earth's axis, and so does not appear to rotate as the Earth rotates in a day. Additionally, when used in the northern hemisphere, the South Pole of a compass needle is attracted to the North Pole of the Earth's magnetic field, so the compass seems to be attracted to Polaris.

A more difficult question is why my wife prefers to hold the map with the lettering the right way up rather than pointing the top of it north but I gather there are two opinions on this matter and mutual incomprehension between the camps.

Nick MacKinnon, Winchester College

In Chile, during the 1980s, road maps produced both by the Servicio Nacional de Turismo-Chile and the oil company Copec all conformed to the convention of having north at the top. At the same time, a series of excellent, more detailed, local guides was produced by the Banco Osorno y Union in Santiago. All the maps and street plans in these guides were orientated with south to the top of the page.

Even in Britain early cartographers did not always put north at the top. A 1716 map of this parish, surveyed for the Duke of Montagu, has south towards the top.

R. Colin Welch, Hemington, Northamptonshire

The Dutch have an excellent (1:200,000) road atlas, half of which shows their country the right way up, and the other half upside-down. It is designed for passengers who, when travelling south, do not think upside-down. Although the atlas is entirely in Dutch, its title is in English: "Upside Down". They must have had us in mind.

Mark Jones, York

The convention of north usually appearing at the top of a map became commonplace during the 17th century. Prior to this, numerous maps had appeared without adhering to this now commonly accepted convention, one of the best known being a sequence of maps of the British Isles "lying on its back" with west to the top of the page published from around 1546 until the 1630s. Often mapmakers would orientate their maps in the most convenient directions to fit the proportions of a folio sheet of paper on which the map was printed. However, as terrestrial globes became widely known as a representation of the world, north at the top became the norm.

Despite this, maps can still be produced defying common practice and so an "Australian's map of the world" might show Australia at the top. Whether such cartographical licence is politically or humorously intended is up to the map maker.

Jonathan Potter, Jonathan Potter Limited (Antique Maps),
London W1

"Upside down" maps showing Australia and Antarctica at the top are freely available in gift shops throughout Australia — more as a statement of Aussie pride/humour, I suspect, than for regular use.

Robin Alexander, Holywood, Co Down

Traditional Chinese maps had East on the left, South on the top, West to the right, and thus North at the bottom.

David Hartill, Cambridge

One does not know whether our Celtic ancestors made maps, but the map in their heads had the east at the top. This would make south the right-hand and north the left-hand.

Old Cornish for south and right-hand is *deghow*, while north and left-hand is *kledh*. Welsh and Breton cognates have the same double meaning. As some of your correspondents indicate, the English got their bearings from the Pole Star, whereas the Britons had looked towards the rising sun.

The Rev John Woods, Much Wenlock, Shropshire

Norman Davies's book *Europe, a History* (Oxford University Press, 1996) contains several maps with Europe standing on its "base" (of the Urals) with west at the top. One is an engraving from an edition of Sebastian Muntzer's 16th-century work, *Cosmography.*

Davies justifies his continued use of this in the book as showing how much more significant the Central and Eastern parts of Europe are than is usually reflected in Western European works. This seems a historical rather than a political or humorous reason but perhaps also fits the page better.

Michael Forrest, Henley-on-Thames

What size do hills have to be to become mountains — or does something else define the difference?

Lucy Stroud (aged 9), London SE1

Although there is no precise international classification of mountains, Ordnance Survey tends to reflect local nomenclature as a way out of the difficulty. In England, Ireland and Wales, the minimum height has been agreed as 2,000ft (610m) but then there are two schools of thought on this.

The first is that every summit over 2,000ft should be regarded as a mountain, but the second maintains that it should have a peak or summit. This means that Kinder Scout (636m) in the Peak District is a mountain in the first case but not in the second, because it lacks an obvious summit and is thus merely high moorland. Nevertheless, Pen-y-ghent in the Yorkshire Dales is certainly a mountain.

Scotland becomes still more complex to satisfy walkers and climbers. Above 2,000ft in the lowlands they are described as Donalds. Grahams come in at 2,000–2,500ft, as long as they have 150ft of descent all around, followed by Corbetts at 2,500–2,999ft. Finally, for the more energetic, Munros start above 3,000ft.

Robert Vincent, Andover, Hampshire

The difference is all in the mind, a matter of use and familiarity, and to some degree, of ease of access.

One speaks of "mountain-climbing" and "hill-walking". But a

famous master mountaineer, Geoffrey Winthrop Young, wrote a book called *On High Hills*, mostly about Alpine peaks of over 14,000ft; and another well-respected book is Carr and Lister's *The Mountains of Snowdonia*, about peaks that never reach as much as 4,000ft.

Few would suggest that the Peak District in Derbyshire contains any mountains. But if you go out on those hills on a winter's afternoon, and it comes on to snow, you will quickly find yourself needing a great deal of mountaineering experience, and mountaineering equipment, if you are not to freeze to death before dark.

Michael Spencer, Dunoon, Argyll

Interesting regional differences in usage apply to hills and mountains across the British Isles. In Scotland, especially the Highlands, "the hill" may refer to anything from relatively low grouse moors and sheep grazings to high deer forests of 3,000ft and more, and even 4,409ft Ben Nevis. "Mountain" is a word seldom used by Scottish farmers or sportsmen, and is a ramblers' and climbers' term.

In Ireland, however, a "mountain" may mean virtually any area of heather, even if it is at or below sea level, and quite flat. Its designation is similar to that of a "moss" in the Scottish Lowlands, and "moss" is often used for "mountain" in the northeastern areas of Ireland settled by 17th-century Scots Planters.

An Irish "mountain" usually demands far less energy to tackle than the often very daunting "hill" in Scotland . . .

Colin McKelvie, Culbokie, Ross-shire

Gilbert White reported in *The Natural History of Selborne* (1789): "The prospect is bounded on the south east and east by the vast range of mountains called the Sussex Downs." They include Mount Caburn and Mount Harry on either side of Lewes, rising to about 600ft.

W. R. P. Bourne, Dufftown, Moray

To the north of Fort William in the Highlands, there is a range of mountains known as The Aonachs.

There are two main mountains: Aonach Beag (translation: "little hill") and Aonach Mor (translation: "big hill"), with respective heights of 1,234m and 1,221m. You will see that the taller is known as little hill, while the shorter is known as big hill. This is because Aonach Mor covers a larger surface area and is much bulkier in shape.

Christopher Horton, Aberlour, Banffshire

In 1765 Richard Hull of Leith Hill in Surrey was determined to own a mountain. He claimed that 1,000ft was the criterion, and as Leith Hill was rather below that height, he built a tower on the summit, which added the necessary number of feet. When he died he was buried beneath his tower — upon his mountain.

I would be saddened if those who have authority over mountains and hills were to overrule Richard's assertion, as I take great pleasure in telling my friends that I regularly cycle to the top of the only mountain in the South of England.

Michael Gleed, Epsom Downs, Surrey

I recently spoke to a soldier posted to the South of England who told me that he rather missed being in the mountains. Having heard that there were mountains in Scotland, he duly resolved to travel there on his next period of leave so as to comfort his eyes with the sight of high, snowy peaks.

He subsequently told me of his travels across the length and breadth of the country but, alas, he had not been able to find the mountains, despite searching everywhere for them.

Without wishing to offend the Scottish mountaineering or tourist board fraternities, I should point out that the said soldier was a Gurkha. The point at which a hill becomes a mountain is surely dependent on the perception of the judge.

Andrew Linehan, Edinburgh

The distinction is neatly explained in the *Longman Family Dictionary*, 1984 edition.

Using this guide, I am informed that a hill is "a rounded natural rise of land lower than a mountain". The same edition goes on to define a mountain as "a landmass that projects conspicuously above its surroundings and is higher than a hill".

I hope this clears up any confusion.

Les Upchurch, Brentwood, Essex

What is the origin of the modern German flag? Before 1945, German flags always consisted of red, white and black (blood, sweat and iron).

Robert Welding, Oxford

When Napoleon was on the retreat from Russia, German students 'ormed volunteer bodies to fight the French. There was no time to make uniforms, so they sewed red trimmings onto black civilian clothes. After the war they sported black and red commemorative badges to which a gold band was added later. At the student demonstrations at the Wartburg in 1817 they flew a red-black-gold flag, which henceforth became the flag of National Unity and Freedom. (Perhaps there was a memory of the Peasants' Revolt in 1525, which had also hoisted a black, red and gold banner.) During the shortlived 1848 revolution, the Frankfurt Assembly adopted black-red-gold as the national flag to symbolise democratic freedom and unity.

With the failure of the 1848 revolution, there was no national flag until northern Germany was united under Prussian leadership in 1866. The Prussian flag — inherited from the Teutonic Knights whose last Grandmaster had been a Hohenzollern — was black and white. The Hohenzollern King of Prussia had originally been Elector of Brandenburg, whose colours were red and white. So the flag of northern, and after 1871, of the whole united Germany became the striped black-white-red.

The Hohenzollerns lost the throne in 1918 and the Weimar Republic, with its very democratic constitution, re-adopted black-red-gold as the national flag. When Hitler overthrew the republic in 1933, he first returned to the striped black-white-red flag as the national flag but ordered it to be flown alongside the swastika, the flag he had personally designed for the Nazi Party. In 1935, when Germany had become a one-party state, he declared the swastika to be the only national flag.

After the war both the West and the East German Governments returned to black-red-gold, although, to distinguish their flag from the West German flag, the East Germans superimposed on the middle band their communist symbol of a hammer and a compass encircled by a wreath of rye. This symbol of course disappeared when West and East Germany were reunited.

Ralph Blumenau, London W11

I was taught as a boy in Hamburg that the present colours came from the motto of the earlier 19th-century student riots: "*Aus schwarzer Nacht fuhrt ein blutiger Pfad zur goldener Freiheit!*" — "From black night leads a bloody path to golden freedom!" Hence: black, red, gold.

Hermann Rohde, Great Yarmouth

How does the Orange mobile phone network advertise itself in Northern Ireland? I can't imagine that either the name, or the slogan "The future's bright, the future's Orange", would go down well in certain parts.

Alex Miller, West Lulworth, Dorset

I've worked for Orange in Belfast for nearly six years and while our name has generated the odd humorous headline, no one in Northern Ireland has ever seriously been confused by thinking the brand anything other than a mobile phone network. We run exactly the same marketing campaigns in Northern Ireland as in the rest of the UK — and that includes the line "The future's bright, the future's Orange".

So, I can confirm that Northern Ireland's future is bright and it is Orange.

Jonathan Rose, Senior Regional PR Manager, Orange UK, Belfast

Orange is actually a very good choice as two of Northern Ireland's leading Gaelic Games teams, Armagh and Antrim, play in that colour. A few years back, large banners all over South Armagh proclaimed the message: "The Future's Bright, The Future's Orange." Armagh went on to win the All Ireland Championship the next year.

M. Murphy, Loughborough

Tim Lemon, the Ulster Unionist candidate for Belfast East at the 2001 general election, attempted to turn this problem to his advantage.

His election posters bore the slogan: "The future's bright, the future's Lemon."

Steve Pomeroy, Cardiff

I was interested to read about Holland and the Netherlands, but where do the "Dutch" come from?

Alan Ardouin, Canterbury

In medieval times the Germanic people with whom the ordinary Englishman most frequently came into contact were sailors who lived on the other side of the North Sea. They probably described themselves as "Deutsch", which was later corrupted in English and written as "Dutch".

In contrast, the "Germanic" people with whom the English aristocracy came into contact were the aristocracy of the Holy Roman Empire. The mutual language of communication that they used was Latin, hence the area from which they came was described as "Germania", which later became "Germany".

To this day, notwithstanding the atrocities of 1940–45, the Dutch national anthem has references to the country's Germanic origin — the opening lines of the anthem (written about 1569) being "*Wilhelmus van Nassouwe / Ben ik van Duitsen bloed*" which translates as: "I am William of Nassau / Of Germanic descent".

Martin Vlietstra, Fleet, Hampshire

From the late Middle Ages to the 16th century, when linguistic distinctions were not sharply defined, the English often described anyone speaking a Germanic language as "Doch" or "T(h)eutonicus", heedless of whether the subject hailed from Antwerp, Hamburg or Nuremburg. A survey of aliens in London in 1568 found 5,225 "Dutch parsons" but only a meagre 22 "Garmans".

Once the northern provinces of the Habsburg Low Countries gained their political independence in the early 17th century, it became usual to distinguish between Dutch and German speakers and their cultures. "Dutch" derives from the Middle Dutch *duuts* or *diets* which ultimately stem from the old Germanic word *theudo*, meaning "people".

The nomenclature for the Low Countries has long puzzled foreigners, and no wonder. In the early modern period there were perhaps eight different ways of referring to the region, its inhabitants and cultures.

Alastair Duke, Southampton

8. FAITH THE FACTS

I have been told that there is only one joke in the whole of the Bible. Can anyone enlighten me?

Geoffrey Bard, Stanmore, Middlesex

Cain's response to God's question as to the whereabouts of the sheep-keeping Abel, "I know not; Am I my brother's keeper?" is perhaps the first joke in the Bible, but is in questionable taste, as he has just murdered him.

Simon Congdon, London EC3

If jokes depend on irony, incongruity or paradox, then the Bible is full of jokes. The story of Balaam's ass (Numbers xxii) is certainly funny. Similarly, the prophets of the Old Testament often did strange things, like eating scrolls (Ezekiel iii) and hiding underwear under rocks (Jeremiah xiii).

Jesus has a particular eye for the ironical and paradoxical. He gave His Disciples nicknames: Peter, the Rock, who was big on words (but a coward when it mattered); James and John, hotheads, were "Sons of Thunder". He told stories about judges who gave justice only after being pestered repeatedly, businessmen who amassed riches only to die the next day, and about priests too precious to help a man who had been beaten up. He talked about people who gave stones in the place of bread, and saw the speck in the eye of another but ignored the log in their own eye. He talked about the blind leading the blind. He called the holy men of His day "whitewashed walls". Some of this, surely, raised a laugh.

But best of all was His entry into Jerusalem, as Messiah, the warrior king, with the crowds cheering, on the back not of a charger, but a donkey. Pure Python.

Father Peter Weatherby, Stoke-on-Trent

There are actually plenty of jokes in the Bible; certainly stories that would make the hearers laugh (the Bible was initially intended to be read aloud to a gathered audience). Many of His comments would have had His live audience in stitches too, while, at the same time, making a deep point. The picture painted of the "blind Pharisees" in

Matthew xxiii, 24, "straining at a gnat but swallowing a camel" is hilarious. Similarly it is reckoned that shepherds were the butt of Galilean society's jokes, and so the one about the shepherd in Luke xv leaving the 99 to search for just one would also have raised a laugh.

George Newton, Aldershot, Hampshire

One of your cor respondents thinks the one about leaving the 99 sheep to look for the one is a joke. It's no joke, as a retired schools inspector from Yorkshire described on Radio 4 some years ago.

He told the class about the parable, thinking to explain care for the wanderer, but a young pupil from an agricultural background said: "Ay, it's tup" — ie, the ram, possibly the only ram of the flock.

Philip Seager, Sheffield

What is truth? said jesting Pilate; and would not stay for an answer. That certainly isn't the only one. What about the rib-tickler in John i, 45–46?

Philip: "We have found him, of whom Moses in the law, and the prophets, did write, Jesus of Nazareth, the son of Joseph."

Nathaniel: "Can any good thing come out of Nazareth?"

And of course Christ always had snappy one-liners ready for the occasion, such as "Let the dead bury their dead," and "The poor always ye have with you." It's how you tell them. Try these prefaced with a heavy shrug and "Oy vay."

Adrian Williams, Oxford

It is on the first page and is usually omitted. It reads: "All characters and events in this book are fictitious and any similarity to persons living or dead is entirely accidental".

Sebastian Marr, Chippenham, Wiltshire

Anyone who has suffered at Maine Road can quote the Bible: ". . . that great city" (Revelation xiv, 8), "Woe to the bloody city!" (Nahum iii, 1), and of course: "Jesus looked upon the city. Jesus wept!" (Luke xix, 41).

Bob Ellis, Southport, Lancashire

There are lots of plays on words in the Old Testament but you need to know Hebrew to understand them. My erstwhile rabbi assured me though that there was ice cream in biblical times: Walls of Jericho and Lyons of Judah.

Barry Hyman, Bushey Heath, Hertfordshire

During Ramadan, Muslims fast from sunrise to sunset. Is any adjustment made for those living in very high latitudes? As the fast comes in winter, Ramadan sounds pretty easy for a Muslim living in the far north, for sunset and sunset are only a few hours apart. If no allowances are made, life must be intolerable for those living in far southern latitudes where Ramadan occurs in their summer — and indeed impossible within the Antarctic circle, where the Sun will never set.

David Stevenson, Newport on Tay, Fife

One must bear in mind that the Hijri calendar is lunar: all dates advancing 11 days a year against the Gregorian calendar. Thus, the current easy northern fast and difficult southern one will reverse in a few years. Ease and difficulty of fasting during Ramadan evens out over time.

The question of perpetual light or darkness in polar regions received a good deal of attention when I lived in Saudi Arabia a few years ago. During one Ramadan, there was a Saudi scientist in Antarctica and a Saudi astronaut in orbit. Either could have deferred the fast until returning home, on the ground that they were travellers, but they chose instead to observe the fasting hours of their home cities.

N. F. Parker, London W2, www.MiddleEastAdvice.com

When was the first recorded incidence of one party professing to be Christian killing another also claiming to be Christian in a dispute over dogma?

J. Davies, London SE24

I would offer the case of Priscillian, Bishop of Avila, in the late 4th century.

He was a layman who embraced a form of Manichaean dualism, the belief that the principle of evil exists in permanent independence of the principle of good.

Although his doctrines were condemned by the Spanish Church in AD380, two bishops consecrated him Bishop of Avila soon afterwards.

In AD381 his opponents had him exiled from Spain. Appeals to Pope Damasus and St Ambrose of Milan were unsuccessful but the Emperor Gratian authorised his return to Avila.

In AD383 Gratian was murdered by the usurper Magnus Maximus, military commander in Britain. He was recognised by Theodosius, the eastern Augustus, as ruler from Trier of Gaul and Spain as well as Britain. Maximus seems, as an orthodox Catholic and a Spaniard, to have come under pressure from the Church to deal with Priscillian, and a Council was called at Bordeaux (AD384) which condemned Priscillian and his followers. They appealed to Magnus at Trier but were accused of sorcery in the civil courts. Despite the protests of St Martin of Tours, Priscillian was executed. This set an evil precedent for using the civil power to settle an ecclesiastical row by violence.

Priscillianism lingered on in Spain well into the Visigothic period. Magnus Maximus was defeated in battle by Theodosius and executed in AD388.

Robin Birch, Oxford

Further to the previous answer, attributing it to the year AD384, Henry Chadwick, in the *The Early Church*, records that in AD370 a deputation of clergy protesting against the appointment of Demophilus (a follower of the Arian heresy) as Bishop of Constantinople was burnt to death. According to Chadwick, both Demophilus and his Arian predecessor, Eudoxius, were supported by the Eastern emperor, Valens, and those who refused communion with Eudoxius and Demophilus were subjected to sporadic persecution.

Brian Bagot, Cranleigh, Surrey

Assuming that one is fortunate enough to be allowed into Heaven, how does one then pass the time?

Arthur Harada, Chester

Eating foie gras to the sound of trumpets was good enough for Sydney Smith. Who am I to disagree with such an eminent cleric?

Michael Forrest, Henley-on-Thames

Counting one's blessings, I would think.

Owen Luder, Laugharne, Carmarthenshire

Considering that modern physics indicates that linear time is an illusion that is peculiar to our limited three-dimensional perception of the Universe, I think it is safe to assume that Heaven is beyond our limited experience, and that the concept of time simply does not apply there.

Philip Hibbs, Birmingham

As one of your original correspondents intimated, the conventional answer is that there is no time to pass: you would be in eternity, which is not an infinite time but a state in which time does not pass.

However, if this turns out to be wrong, you could try signing up for the heavenly choir. A tone-deaf person like myself could spend several millennia learning to sing sweetly, ditto for playing the harp. Then there are the flying lessons: I'd have a bit of an advantage there, having flown light aircraft, but for the majority of newly fledged angels this could take a while. You have to be able to fly in perfect formation, playing the harp and singing Handel's *Messiah*, before you get your wings.

David Joslin, Acklam, North Yorkshire

In the Jewish tradition, Heaven will be a place of great study, with God as the teacher, and banquets. Happily, Heaven is not restricted to Jews but will include all the righteous people of the world.

Rabbi Douglas Charing, Leeds

Your correspondent's intimations of boredom are supported by words in a famous hymn: "Then, like stars his children crowned / All in white shall wait around".

J. B. Sturton, Bedford

This brings to mind the story of the man on his deathbed being asked if he had any questions regarding his time after death. He asked: "Do they play darts in Heaven? As that has been my sole enjoyment on Earth." The parson replied that he would do his best to find out and tell him his findings.

A few days later he called to announce he had good and bad news. The good news was: "Yes, they do play darts in Heaven."

"The bad news is that you are in next Wednesday's team."
John Heath, Ipswich

One would probably go crazy with boredom. As Mark Twain once observed, all the really interesting people are down below: "So there you have it. Heaven for climate; Hell for society."
Philip Yaffe, Brussels

A friend was recently preparing for her imminent death from cancer. As she was someone who had always been busy, something which was taxing her was "this eternity thing". However her mind was put to rest by a fellow Roman Catholic, who stated that it would take an eternity for there to be women priests in their Church, so perhaps she could work on that.
Lesley Tregaskes, Cobham, Surrey

I once heard a sermon at Brompton Oratory which suggested that being in Heaven is like permanently attending Solemn Vespers as it is celebrated in that church.

Should your correspondent require a rehearsal for eternal life, he has only to go to the Oratory at 3.30pm every Sunday afternoon for a foretaste.
Ian Wells, Nottingham

The Roman Catholic Church's Brompton Oratory does not have the monopoly on giving an insight into what Heaven is like. In his autobiography *The No-nonsense Vicar* (1995), Father Derek White describes solemn evensong and benediction at Holy Trinity, Gosport, back in the great Father Cyril Barclay's time in the Seventies, as what he "imagined Heaven to be like".
The Rev R. H. North Kerr, Kingston upon Thames

Larry King once asked Sylvia Brown, the well-known American psychic, this very same question. Her reply was that "up there", one occupies oneself with pursuits such as gardening and animal husbandry.

This immediately put me off ever trying to get there. But I was happy for my beloved late aunt, who all her life loved gardening, and my much loved sister, who is a dab hand at breeding champion show-jumping ponies. She was delighted when I told her that she will be able to continue with this favourite pastime indefinitely.

Penelope Gale, Cirencester

God knows.

Mike Gregory, Caithness

When and why did the Gideons start putting Bibles in hotel rooms?

Richard Martin, London SW8

The Gideons International have been placing Bibles in hotels since 1908.

Why? Because we believe the Bible is God's Word and we want to make it freely available so that people can read how God intended we should live, and that we might have a relationship with God.

Ken Neilson, Executive Secretary, Gideons International,
Lutterworth, Leicestershire

My great-grandfather, George Vigeon (d. 1873), was the founding secretary of the Commercial Travellers Christian Association. He was a devout Methodist layman much involved in inner-city mission in London. He was very concerned for the spiritual welfare of commercial travellers who would leave home on Sunday night and take train to their area of operation for the coming week, spending their evenings propping up the bars of seedy commercial "railway" hotels. He conceived the idea of putting Bibles in bedrooms in these hotels and was, I believe, the pioneer of such evangelical initiatives. The Gideons, of course, were founded a generation or so later.

The story goes that George visited New York in 1873 as a fraternal delegate to the annual conference of the American Evangelical Alliance, and was much entertained and feted by his American hosts. I like to think that he shared his vision of a Bible in every bedroom on that occasion and that, in typical fashion, it was American business-men who latched on to that idea and made it the international enterprise it is today.

My son has the Bible which was presented to George on that occasion by President Ulysses Grant, and we have letters which he wrote to his wife describing his experiences: "everything is so big in America" he wrote, "especially the cemeteries!"

Canon Owen Vigeon (retd), Bromsgrove, Worcestershire

What are today's seven deadly sins?

Bill Coles, Edinburgh

Intolerance
Apathy
Greed
Impatience
Envy
Dogmatism
Complacency

M. K. Williams, High Wycombe, Buckinghamshire

Patriotism
Elitism
Reason
Decorum
Obedience
Loyalty
Efficiency

Netta Goldsmith, Tunbridge Wells

9. LIFE MATTERS

Who owns the copyright to the graffiti drawn on my wall?
David Toft, Runcorn, Cheshire

Assuming that the graffiti meet the minimum requirements for qualifying for copyright protection as an artistic or literary work (depending on the nature of the graffiti), the first owner of the copyright will be the graffiti artist. It is likely to be implied that the artist has made a gift to the homeowner of the paint applied to the wall of his home, but that will not give the homeowner a licence to reproduce the work elsewhere (unless he can obtain the permission of the artist).
Tim Bamford, London EC4

The graffiti "artist" could not establish copyright as he, presumably, used the wall without the owners' permission. You cannot obtain copyright by unlawful means. A tort has been committed so the owner of the wall could sue the graffitist for the cost of the removal of his "creation".
Peter Windle, Newcastle upon Tyne

Why do we drive on the left hand side of the road and when did the practice become compulsory for coaches and then cars?
Andrew Hoare, Liverpool

We drive on the left because we are (predominantly) right-handed. A man with a sword by his side will find it easier to mount a horse from the left, so avoiding the need to throw the sword over the horse as he mounts. Thus the convention of standing to the left of your horse or carriage was formed. The more interesting question is why so many countries drive on the right — surely they can't have been predominantly left-handed swordsmen?
Pete Ansbro, Bury St Edmunds

The Romans were the first to institute a formal rule of the road that stipulated driving on the left. This remained common practice in Europe until Napoleon decided to switch to the right in France to be different from Britain, and imposed this on the territories that he conquered. America drives on the right due to a similar decision taken during the War of Independence. So the worldwide predominance of driving on the right is simply due to a desire not to be governed by British rules of the road.

Mark Goodge, Cambridge

As to the notion that the War of Independence led the Americans to introduce right hand drive as an anti-British move, your correspondent should take a look at photographs of the Civil War, and see which side of the road the Confederates were driving and riding on in the 1860s. It was on the left, and remained so until the introduction of the Model T Ford, with its steering wheel on the left. This was contrary to almost all previous cars (including the very first car in Germany) which had their steering wheels on the right.

Dan Parker, Cobham, Surrey

I recall an article some years ago reporting on an archaeological dig, which suggested that the practice of driving on the left was established during the Roman occupation of Britain. The site in question had been used as a quarry and carts entering and leaving had left ruts in the mud. Those ruts on the left of the entrance (looking from the inside out) were deeper than those on the right suggesting that the carts leaving (and laden with stone) had been driven on the left.

Simon East, Bristol

Bruce Watson, Senior Archaeologist at the Museum of London, states that as far as he knows the first documented evidence of a keep-left rule was the appointment of three men by the Court of Common Council of the City of London to direct traffic to the left side of London Bridge in 1722.

D. W. Laing, Co. Antrim

An exensive study of the side of the road used by all the countries of the world and the theories of how the differences came about can be found on the Net at: http://www.travel-library.com/general/driving/drive_which_side.html#listofcountries.

Ralph Gabriel, Chobham

Why are nearly all caravans white, or a boring beige colour? Why are they not made in a variety of colours, like cars?

Wendy Hillary, Chinnor, Oxfordshire

Caravans in neutral-ish colours won't clash too badly with the towing vehicle. Therefore, the caravan manufacturers please more of the people more of the time because neither the colour of the car nor the caravan enters the equation when it comes to choice. Also, caravanners are relieved of a potential colour quandary when it comes to changing their car but keeping their caravan. Black is also neutral but, with so many flat panels, every dent, "ding" and bit of grot would be very visible as anyone who has ever had a black car will testify. Personally, I will never, ever have a caravan, no matter what the colour scheme.

Aran Wood, London N8

Some years ago, after owning two commercially made caravans, I decided to design my own, and had it finished in a dark olive green so that it would merge with the countryside. In sunny weather it was like an oven. My knowledge of physics should have told me that white surfaces absorb much less heat from the sun, and conversely lose much less when internal heating has to be used in cold weather. Consequently, white vans are far more pleasant and economical to use.

Roy Hardley, St Helens, Lancashire

Why do clocks with Roman numerals always display 4 as IIII rather than IV?

John Sayers, Liverpool

This goes back to the time of Charles II, who liked to play about with clocks. He made the error of recording the Roman numeral IV as IIII. No one had the nerve to tell him he had made a mistake.

Bernard Parke, Guildford

Your correspondent says that Charles II "made the error of recording the Roman numeral IV as IIII". Precedent is seen in the legionary coins struck for Mark Antony where among deviations from our expectation we also find IIX, VIIII, XIIII, XIIX, and XVIIII.

The Rev K.V. Hewitt, Bromley, Kent

There is no question of Charles II getting it wrong by using IIII.
   Although we no longer regard it as normative, IIII (or iiij in later

manuscripts) was in fact the "earlier" form of four in Roman numerals. Similarly, nine was VIIII, fourteen XIIII, nineteen XVIIII etc. So far as we are able to tell, these forms continued to be exclusively used throughout the Saxon period.

Karl Wittwer, Maidstone

Clocks with Roman numerals always display 4 as IIII because it is aesthetically more pleasing, for it balances the number VIII on the opposite side of the face.

Malcolm S. Bermange, Radlett, Hertfordshire

Because they appear at an angle round a circle, this is to avoid confusion with VI. But note that Big Ben does not follow this rule.

Peter Bicknell, Thorncombe, Somerset

Why are young children always attracted to walking along the top of low walls?

H. Nightingale, Surbiton, Surrey

Experiencing elements of controlled fear is a well-accepted form of human gratification. This is because the adrenalin produced when doing so produces an element of excitement and pleasure, especially immediately after the experience.

In proportion to their height and therefore their own perception, for small children the wall is very high. Often with a parent present the perfect combination of safety and excitement is created. This would be very similar to the enthusiasm for a trip to the playground to play on something like a swing or a slide, the excitement of which should never be underestimated by an adult.

Jack Edmondson, Gloucester

It is probably in unappreciated fulfilment of a desire to be as tall as the grown-ups.

Paul Motte-Harrison, Shoreham-by-Sea, West Sussex

Is there a legitimate patron saint of gardening? We wish to dedicate a granite folly we are building.

Dr and Mrs P. E. Kapff, Newton Abbot, Devon

The patron saint of gardeners is St Fiacre. This saint was born in

Ireland and lived in the town of Kilfiachra in Co. Kilkenny but travelled, in 628, to France in search of greater solitude. In France he was granted, by the Bishop of Mieux, St Faro, as much land as he could surround in one day with a furrow. Fiacre dug the furrow with the point of his crozier. Here he founded a monastery where he lived a life of fast, prayer, vigil and manual labour in his garden.

St Fiacre is also the patron saint of cab-drivers, particularly Parisian cabbies. This arises from the fact that the first place to allow coaches to ply for hire in Paris was the Hotel St-Fiacre in the Rue St-Martin.

Stephen Ringer, Flimwell, East Sussex

St Dorothea, virgin and martyr, is the patron saint of gardeners. Born in Caesarea she was martyred under Diocletian. Brought before the Roman governor, she refused to apostosise and welcomed her martyrdom as she would soon be in the gardens of Paradise. There are stained glass windows in her honour in the churches of Roxton, Bedfordshire, and North Elmham, Norfolk.

Dorothea Sheppard, Llansantffraid, Powys

The patron of gardeners is Saint Gertrude of Nivelles (626–659). Fine weather on her feast day, March 17, is your signal to begin spring planting.

Martin Stevens, London SE11

Other candidates are saints Adelard, Tryphon and Phocas. I cannot find a patron saint for follies; I expect he or she belonged to the other side.

Mark Powlson, Ashtead, Surrey

As the project is the construction of a concrete folly, I suggest either St Simon Stylites, the Elder (c.390–459), who lived for 37 years up a stone pillar; or the unrelated St Simon Stylites, the Younger (521–597), who was up aloft for 68 years. There is also St Barbara, a beautiful maiden imprisoned in a high tower by her father, and whose patronage embraces architects, builders, construction workers and stone masons.

Jim McCormack, Dublin

St James of Compostella.

Rosena Hynes, Leeds

Like a million others, I have rededicated my compost heap to St Alan.

Anthony Aust, London W6

With the potential onset of balmy weather, our thoughts may turn to sitting in the garden or on a terrace quaffing Pimm's No 1 (gin-based) or No 6 (vodka based). But what happened to Pimm's numbers 2, 3, 4 and 5?

Andrew Barnett, London N4

Some years ago I wrote to Pimm's Ltd and asked them the same question. I cannot do better than relay you the words of their reply, letter dated September 14, 1994.

"There were for a number of years prior to the Second World War and up to 1964 four Pimm's Cups. In that year Nos 5 and 6 were added to the range, the base spirits of which were, in numerical order, gin, whisky, brandy, rum, rye whisky and vodka.

"The decision was taken in 1972 to discontinue Nos 2 to 6 as, in total, their sales represented less than 5 per cent of our business, and also it was felt that their existence created some confusion in the consumer's mind as to what Pimm's is.

"In 1977, in response to a small but persistent demand, the No 6 Cup was reintroduced as Pimm's Cup Vodka Base, but its sales are still relatively small — less than 2.5 per cent of our total business — and it is not readily obtainable from all wine and spirit retail outlets."

John Fenwick, Solihull

How do the police, organisers and reporters arrive at their respective estimate of the number of people attending a rally, demonstration, protest or any other large gathering? The estimates rarely agree.

Ernest Danzig, Watford, Hertfordshire

At one time, *The Guinness Book of Records* listed the Jacob Formula as a means of counting crowds. According to this formula, the area allowance per person varies from 4 sq ft (tight) to $9\frac{1}{2}$ sq ft (loose).

This saves one from having to rely on either police figures, usually an underestimate, or the exaggerated numbers claimed by rally organisers.

Tim Mickleburgh, Grimsby

In the 1960s, when I was a staff reporter on *The Daily Express*, I regularly covered the Durham Miners' Gala — the annual Big Meetin'

— then regarded as the free world's biggest trade demonstration. One year I asked the late Alec Muir, then County Durham's Chief Constable, for his estimate of the crowd.

Immediately he replied: "Four hundred and twenty six thousand, three hundred and eighty two." When I asked how he could be so precise he said: "Quite easy, I counted the legs and divided by two." He would not comment further — and was furious when my newspaper reported his comments verbatim. After that he refused to speak to me ever again.

During my many years as a reporter, I had a simple yardstick for estimating large crowds. I knew how many people it took to fill the Gallowgate End at Newcastle United FC's old ground and I compared that in my mind's eye with the area covered by a large rally or demonstration.

Other yardsticks used include:

Organisers of a protest or rally first take an "intelligent" guess at the crowd size — then double it.

If the gathering is anti-law and order, police also make an "intelligent" guess — then halve it.

Stanley Blenkinsop, Macclesfield, Cheshire

Is there an unofficial form of national identity numbering? I've often been puzzled to find a number (77151) against my name and address on a variety of correspondence ranging from official gubbins to junk mail. But now I see it's on my tax form and my car registration.

Gillian Kempster, Chobham, Surrey

The five-digit number is the mailsort number, and comes about because the Royal Mail offers a discount to large customers who pre-sort their mail. The first three digits represent a fairly coarse geographical area (eg, Sheffield) and the full five digits represent the local sorting office (eg, central Chesterfield).

The barcode, which appears on some mail, is an encoding of the postcode and a three-character delivery point suffix that uniquely identifies the premises and allegedly allows the Royal Mail to sort the mail into the individual postman's walksort sequence.

Charles Gaskell, Sheffield Mailsort number 052739

Why must port wine always be passed clockwise and why is it such bad luck to break the chain? I do not have the answer to this, nor have I ever met anyone who does — even very senior naval staff.

Roderick Bromley, Coltishall, Norfolk

There is no mystery here, as any butler knows. All wine is served from the right, here wine glasses are located, but first to the host, who acts as wine taster. Rotation ends with the guest of honour, on the right. Food, on the other hand, is served first to the guest of honour, from his left, avoiding the wine glasses, and rotates anti-clockwise, terminating modestly with the host.

More vitally, when port is served from the bottle, rather than from a decanter, it must be poured delicately with the label up, to confirm that dregs have not been disturbed from the orientation in storage. Any fine wine is insulted if decanted otherwise, and the wise host will refuse to taste it.

As for the bad luck involved in breaking the drinking chain, or any other shipboard chain for that matter — surely no red-blooded sailor needs this explained!

Gerald Stonehill, Denham, Buckinghamshire

You will no doubt receive many explanations for the traditional clockwise movement of port, some buttressed by fantastical legend. Let common sense prevail. The host pours a glass for the guest of honour, who sits on his right. He then pours a glass for himself. There is now only one direction in which the bottle, or decanter, can politely go . . . to the left.

John Graham, London W9

One passes port clockwise because if one were to pass it anti-clockwise one would merely be passing it back to the person who had already passed it to one.

Andy Rodgers, Sheffield

Various possible explanations have been put forward over the years for this, including the direction of rotation of the Earth, the naval connection and even occult suggestions but the answer is very simple: it is easier.

To be correct, the host will pour "back-handed" to the guest on his (or her) right, serve himself and then the decanter circulates clockwise, never stopping until it reaches the host again. As most people are right-handed, this is easier than passing it anti-clockwise. An attentive host will keep an eye out in case any glass is getting dry, in which case he or she will start the decanter off again or, if the party is a large one, the decanter will never stop, even at the head of the table.

Like all the best points of etiquette, the rule stems from common sense. Sticking to the "rules" ensures that everyone is well supplied. If the decanter stops too long in front of a particular diner there are various calls that will go out, the most famous being "Do you know the Bishop of Norwich/Dr Wright?" This usually gets it moving again, but may not work in ecclesiastical or medical circles.

Passing port the wrong way is not bad luck, just bad manners, and manners are taken very seriously in many quarters. I once had lunch at the Factory House in Oporto when a guest passed the decanter the wrong way; no one spoke to him for the rest of the lunch.

Godfrey Spence, author, The Port Companion, *Wine & Spirit Education Trust, London EC4*

Do other countries' railway systems grind to a halt at the onset of autumn owing to a surprise fall of leaves on the line?

Stephen Cuningham, Reading

The simple answer is "yes", but the public, press and media do not make a fuss about it. Just as wet leaves on a pavement can cause loss of footing, they can cause steel wheels to lose firm contact with steel rails.

In Paris, commuters on some lines are only too aware of autumn leaves on the line. The Dutch know the problem as well and have been experimenting with the "Sandite" used in this country. In Germany the Munich Stadtbahn usually gets stitched up at this time of year — yes, leaves again. And only the other week on the Oberammergau branch, the brand-new trains had to be taken off as they cannot cope with . . . leaves on the line.

Thirty years ago in Sweden it was not unknown for a special banking locomotive to be positioned at Norrkoping station to help southbound trains to start away in autumn, because of the number of trees near the station.

The problem has worsened everywhere as we have become "greener".

There were not as many trees and bushes along railway lines years ago — steam locomotives regularly set fire to embankments and this helped to keep things under control. However, even in those far-off days it was not unknown for freight trains to take less tonnage in autumn when adhesion conditions were bad.

Brian Garvin, Beckenham, Kent

What is the origin of drinking a toast and why do we feel the need to say "cheers" or similar before the first sip of an alcoholic drink in company?

Philip Arkell, Winchcombe, Gloucestershire

From very early human times, communities have felt a need to regard their most potent (usually most alcoholic) drink as sacred and to perform some special rite just before it is consumed. Consumption might be only by a celebrant (a shaman or priest, perhaps), but might also be permitted to the members of the tribe or "congregation" present. It would follow a formulaic dedication intended to invoke lasting health and/or prosperity upon the group. Holy rituals of at least two major current religions still contain elements of this practice.

In Mediterranean and Near Eastern communities, probably from the late first half of the first millennium BC, the custom was to dip a piece of dry biscuit-like bread into the sacred beverage at the time of this dedication, and consume it too. During Roman times, such a morsel was described as *tostus*: "baked dry". Nearly two millennia later still, that has become both the "toast" in the toaster and the "toast" of the toastmaster (standing in for the original celebrant, though now without any morsel to dip).

Meanwhile, the ritual expression has been formalised and abbreviated in most European languages to near enough a single word that remains suggestive of future health and prosperity: *Sante!* (health), *Salud!* (health), *Slainte!* (health) *Zdorov'ye!* (health), *Egeszsegere!* (to wholeness), *Terveydeks'!* (to health), *Syhatynyza!* (to health), *Skal!* (the future), *Prosit!* (may things improve) and "Cheers!" (for Pete's sake, try not to look so miserable).

Mike Darton, Preston St Mary, Suffolk [01/01/03]

By the days of Charles II, it was the custom to put pieces of toast into tankards of beer in order to improve the flavour.

According to one story, a celebrated beauty of that time was bathing in the Cross Bath, in Bath. One of her admirers is said to have taken a glass of the water in which she was bathing and drunk her health to the assembled company. Another admirer, somewhat the worse for drink, said that he would jump into the water for, "although he liked not the liquor, he would have the toast", meaning, of course, the lady herself.

Dr James Briggs, Bristol

Does life really begin at 40?

Maureen Robinson (aged 39), Belfast

Being 76, I have spent almost half my years past the age of 40, and I wouldn't have missed it for the world. Since my fortieth, I have had two wonderful children whom I have had the privilege of seeing grow to useful maturity — our son, born when I was 46, is now a doctor of biochemistry. I have seen more of the world, made more friends and generally enjoyed life more.

It is said that we are often too busy doing things that are urgent to do the things that are important. In the past 20 years or so I have been able to do things that are important.

Life doesn't begin at 40, it just gets better.

John Bothwell, Frome, Somerset

Two clerics were debating whether life began at conception or birth. A third answered: "Life begins when the mortgage is paid off, the last child has left home and the family dog is dead."

Jane Lawrence, London SW14

Can anyone tell me which property set in Monopoly yields the greatest return on investment?

R. Cook, Birmingham

Based on the assumption that each site within a colour group is developed to the same extent, and calculated on the basis of a property being landed on once only, the best return on investment comes (as every child instinctively knows) from having a hotel on Mayfair.

To achieve the return of £2,000 requires an outlay of £2,750 (£750 to buy the two sites in the group then 5 x £200 x 2 to build a hotel on each) — a return of 73 per cent.

Surprisingly, however, the other site in the group, Park Lane, achieves only 55 per cent when developed with a hotel, and performs at its best with only three houses (which provide a return of 56 per cent). Also surprising is that the best performer after a hotel on Mayfair is a hotel on Whitechapel Road, which generates 73 per cent.

The worst-performing properties are Oxford Street and Regent Street, which together at their best (with four houses each) show a return of 33 per cent.

Whitehall, Pall Mall, The Strand, Fleet Street, Trafalgar Square, Coventry Street, Leicester Square, Regent Street, Oxford Street and Bond Street plus the stations and the utilities are the dogs to avoid, as they never show a return greater than 40 per cent.

Ian Mandley, Christchurch, New Zealand

Without doubt the best set to own is the Vine Street set just before Free Parking. Relatively cheap to buy and develop, it's where the opposition will always land, game after game. That's because people are always going to jail in Monopoly and when you roll your two dice to get out, chances are you'll roll a 6, 8 or 9 and be paying up!

It might not be the biggest fine, but it certainly adds up and it's better odds than Mayfair!

Timmy Mallett, Cookham, Berkshire

Your first correspondent's reckoning does offset against the extortionate charges for landing on Park Lane and Mayfair the lower probability of landing on a set that contains only two properties rather than three.

I adjust for this by summing the rents on both or all three properties in a set and comparing these totals with the total outlays as calculated by your previous correspondent. This also has the merit of answering the original question, which related to property sets, not individual properties.

On this basis, hotels on Park Lane and Mayfair offer a combined return of £3,500 on a total outlay of £2,750, i.e. a yield of 127 per cent. But the comparable yield on Euston Road, The Angel and Pentonville Road is 154 per cent, and even that on Bow Street, Marlborough Street and Vine Street is better at 141.

Rather curiously, hotels on Park Lane and Mayfair are a slightly worse bet than either three or four houses.

Overall best yields are:

1. Hotels on light blues: 154 per cent
2. Hotels on oranges: 141.
3. Three or four houses on dark blues: 128.
4. Hotels on pinks: 124.
5. Three houses on greens: 123.
6. Hotels on yellows: 115.
7. Hotels on browns: 113.
8. Hotels on reds: 109.
9. All four stations: 100.
10. Utilities: 47 (based on an average dice throw of seven).

Richard Vivian, London SW18

The Beatles were rejected by Decca and the Monopoly game was initially written off by Parker Brothers. What other myopic rejections have gone on to achieve spectacular success?

Folorunso Ajayi, Southport, Lancashire

Here's another to add to the list: Pink Floyd. Their early producer, Joe Boyd, worked for Elektra Records (home of The Doors et al) and tried to interest Jac Holzman, Elektra's boss, into signing them. Not interested . . .

When Boyd left Elektra, he tried to get a deal set up with Polydor. They weren't interested either. Eventually the band got a deal with EMI, in 1967, and have stayed with that label to this day.

Matt Johns, Brighton

Your correspondent is incorrect in attributing a myopic rejection of Pink Floyd to Polydor.

I was marketing manager at Polydor in 1967 and along with the MD, Roland Rennie, negotiated a deal to bring Pink Floyd to the label. We had a handshake on it in my office with the Pink Floyd management. They then went around the corner to Manchester Square, to visit EMI, who trumped our deal on the spot. Joe Boyd can confirm this.

We were more than a little aggrieved. In retrospect, I guess we shouldn't complain, as they were about the only happening band of the day that got away from us . . .

Alan Bates, London SW13

There was a young working-class carpenter who was sentenced to death for blasphemy against the national religion; suspected of treasonable activities against the State; deserted by his supporters and betrayed by his closest friends, and who was nailed up alive by hands and feet to die mocked by the mob.

He is now worshipped by nearly a third of humanity as the embodiment of God.

Paul Murphy, Englefield Green, Surrey

Having had my first novel rejected so far by eight publishers, I comfort myself with the thought that *The Day of the Jackal* by Frederick Forsyth was rejected by a dozen publishers before finally being accepted by the first one who had declined it.

Richard Henwood, Totnes, Devon

I admire the innocence of Richard Henwood, whose first novel has been rejected by eight publishers. Only eight! I have written five novels and been rejected by several hundred if not a thousand publishers and literary agents. And in rejecting my work they have, almost without exception, been rude and dismissive.

The only certain way to get published is to commit a well-publicised crime, then wait for the world to beat a path to your door, contracts in hand. When you read about my crime (probably inflicted upon some literary agent), please go out and buy my book afterwards.

Reginald Tripp, Alton, Hampshire

Publishers didn't exactly rush to accept any of the Brontë novels. *The Professor*, *Wuthering Heights* and *Agnes Grey* were rejected by publishers before acceptance. Charlotte, writing letters to publishers under the name of Currer Bell, didn't even bother to rewrap the parcel when she finally sent *The Professor* to Messrs Smith & Elder. She simply scored out the last address and wrote in the new one. Not unreasonably, George Smith noted: "It was clear that we were offered what had been already rejected elsewhere."

Jane Lawrence, London SW14

The most striking recent example that springs to mind is the Harry Potter book, which was rejected by eight publishers before being taken up by Bloomsbury.

On a different plane, proposals in 1967 by Philip Emeagwali for an internet were rejected by IBM. But years later, after his paper on the subject had won the Gordon Bell Prize, his ideas were vindicated.

Michael Knight, Geneva

One of the most myopic rejections was IBM's attitude to the personal computer when it was first developed in the 1980s. At that time IBM considered the PC to be a non-strategic "entry-level product", believing that most PC purchasers would quickly realise that they needed the serious computing power of IBM's blue boxes.

As the PC was not regarded as a strategic product, IBM contracted a small company known as Microsoft to write the operating system for its PC. By the time that IBM realised its mistake, Microsoft had built an unassailable lead and the rest is history: Microsoft went on to become a force whose profits dwarf those of IBM.

William Chapman, Camberley, Surrey

A correspondent cites IBM's rejection of the personal computer in the early 1980s.

At the time, the US Government was threatening to break up IBM because it had a near-monopoly in computing. If IBM had gained a monopoly over the operating system for the PC, it would have greatly aggravated the situation, so it was careful not to do so. The monopoly has caused Microsoft a lot of trouble in the same way.

Brian Gilbert, Hampton, Middlesex

One of the mainstays of modern diagnostic imaging in medicine is the X-ray CT or CAT scan. Sir Godfrey Hounsfield and Alan Cormack received the Nobel Prize for Medicine or Physiology in 1979 for its invention.

However, Hounsfield acknowledges that in previous work of which at the time he was unaware, an American neurologist called Bill Oldendorf had developed the principles required for X-ray CT. Oldendorf patented his ideas in the early 1960s (ten years before Hounsfield), but his device was met with derision and he was even booed off stage at a scientific meeting.

Perhaps the most myopic comment, though, came from the company he approached with his idea. It replied: "Even if it could be made to work as you suggest, we cannot imagine a significant market for such an expensive apparatus, which would do nothing but make a radiographic cross-section of a head."

Tell that to the staff on *ER* . . .

Dale Bailey, Sydney

When advised of the invention of the telephone and its potential for communication, the chief engineer of the GPO sometime in the 1890s is reported to have replied: "We don't need the telephone; we have plenty of messenger boys."

Brian Winton, Crawley, West Sussex

When I joined the GPO in the 1960s, I was told that after attending an early demonstration of wireless telegraphy the Chief Engineer of the Post Office commented: "The effect demonstrated by Signor Marconi is certainly remarkable, but given the efficiency of the existing telegraph system it can have no practical application."

Michael Baker, Rickmansworth, Hertfordshire

As a rejection not of a single idea or product but of the whole concept of continual advancement, may I nominate Charles H. Duell, US Commissioner of Patents. In 1899 he was reported to have said: "Everything that can be invented has been invented."

H. J. Khang, London SE1

I know about the other three, but what could you listen to at 16rpm on old record players?

Matthew Rosedon, Broadstairs, Kent

16rpm recordings were primarily used for spoken words. In 1932 the United States Government began its "Talking Books for the Blind" programme, recording books and magazines on 16rpm records. The slow speed enabled more material to be recorded.

The sound quality was about the same as a telephone. With the introduction of the audiocassette in 1963, the recording of books moved from records to tape.

Joe Luchok, Arlington, Virginia

It is surprising that thousands of record-players and radiograms were manufactured in the 1950s and 1960s which were capable of playing

16²/₃rpm discs, when so few records at this speed were issued. Although achieving playing times in excess of two hours, 12in 16²/₃rpm LPs revolved too slowly to reproduce music at adequate quality. A small number of speech records were issued in this format but even record companies such as Argo and Caedmon, which specialised in poetry and drama records, released discs which played at 33¹/₃rpm, as they often needed to include musical interludes in their productions.

David Phillips, Margate, Kent

Nor were there only four speeds: my parents had a wax recording of John McCormack's songs which was to be played at 81rpm. The wind-up gramophone was equipped with a mechanical dial which allowed adjustment between 77 and 82rpm.

Edwin Cox, London SE4

My father had a 16rpm record. On one side was the air raid "alert" siren and on the other the "all clear". Each side ran for two minutes. I've no idea as to why it was 16rpm; I only know that as a small boy I took great delight in playing it at full volume at 78rpm. What a nuisance I must have been.

Tim Bower, Aylsham, Norfolk

I never bought a 16rpm record, but made an unexpected discovery as a result of this capability.

There is a Pink Floyd track called *Several Species of Small Furry Animals Gathered Together in a Cave and Grooving with a Pict.* Towards the end, there is a chipmunk-like speeded-up voice, and at 33rpm it is impossible to hear what it is saying. However, at 16rpm, it is quite clear. It says: "That was pretty avant-garde, wasn't it?"

Nicely tongue-in-cheek . . .

Ian Currie, Oxford

How and why did the monocle come to be a symbol of haughtiness and social superiority? Did inbreeding among the upper classes lead to a genetic defect which affected only one eye?

Richard Need, Cheam, Surrey

There are claims that the Roman Emperor Nero was first to have a monocle when he used a single eyeglass cut from emerald to reduce the Sun's glare as he watched gladiators in the arena. The monocle as we know it today, however, dates back to the 18th century, when it developed from spectacles in France, Germany and Britain. The main reasons for its development was that people with only weak eye saw little point in having a lens for each.

Making a proper monocle was costlier than producing a pair of spectacles. This was because the monocle was individually made to fit the bone structure of the face between eyebrow, cheek and nose. So monocles gradually became identified with the wealthy and ruling classes. Writers such as P. G. Wodehouse reinforced this in his novels and also his "Rules for novelists" with its clause on monocles: "These may be worn by good dukes and all Englishmen. No bad man wears a monocle."

Because they were very popular in the senior ranks of the German Army of the First World War, they became identified with militarism. In the Zulu Wars of the late 19th century, the Zulus described monocle-wearing British Army officers as "men with three eyes". At Gallipoli in 1915 a monocled British major was inspecting Australian soldiers. As he approached, several of them put a silver coin in one eye. In reply the office took out his monocle, flicked it like a coin high above the trench parapet as the Turkish bullets whistled overhead and expertly caught it back in his eye, at which point the Anzacs gave him a standing ovation.

According to opticians there is no proof that inbreeding among the upper classes led to a genetic defect affecting only one eye. They say that many people have eyes of different power. I am not haughty, socially superior or inbred, but I have happily and usefully worn a monocle for almost 40 years — the first of them provided free by the NHS.

Stanley Blenkinsop, Macclesfield, Cheshire

Why is the meat sold in supermarkets so rubbery?

Lawrence Frewin, London SW12

This is because much of this meat is rushed from farm to processing plant and then to supermarkets without being allowed to hang properly or for long enough. The meat sold in my local farm shop has been hung for between 14 and 28 days, and that in my butcher's for 28 days.

The hanging process allows the meat to mature and for it to be broken down by enzymes. This tenderises the meat and removes "rubberiness". It also gives the meat a darker, dryer texture. Most supermarket customers will be used to buying their bright red meat in polystyrene packets, which often contain a lot of moisture.

My advice to anyone who is sick of this state of affairs is to seek out a well-established butcher or farm shop. You may pay a little extra for your meat but at least it will be tender and taste of something.

Austin Muscatelli, Nedderton, Northumberland

Why do women wear high heels?

Paul Anderson, Loughborough

Every fashionista and sensible woman knows that high heels make your legs look thinner and longer. Enough said!

Sarah Stanford, Slough

Many short women wear high heels simply to look taller; a girlfriend of mine certainly did. But if you took a poll among men, I would guess you would find that most like to see women in heels, as it makes them appear more attractive.

Elsewhere, females sometimes want to project a kind of image when they are not trying to attract the opposite sex, and being taller helps them to feel powerful. I mean, how many ladies of influence do you see in flatties or — perish the thought — training shoes?

Tim Mickleburgh, Grimsby

High heels were invented by short women who were tired of being kissed on the forehead.

Archie Thomson, Whitby, North Yorkshire

Has anyone ever used a pair of women's tights to replace temporarily a broken fan belt and get a car moving again?

Richard Oakman, Penarth, Vale of Glamorgan

Some years ago in the mid-1970s I was returning home in my Mini from Oxford. I reached Nottingham when my car simply overheated and then gave out on me.

Fortunately, two lovely policemen were passing in their panda car and asked if I needed help. After looking under the bonnet, one of them asked me if I was wearing tights. Although it did cross my mind as to why they had asked, I said that I was.

I was then requested to remove them (in a suitably discreet manner) and the deed was done. I was sent off to a garage not too far away where the proprietor fortunately had one fan belt to fit a Mini and did the job there and then.

The substitution does work — for a few miles, at least.

Mary Ellis, Lincoln

On Christmas Eve 1950 after my Morris Minor fan belt broke, my friend and I were left stranded in the Ituri Forest on Uganda's border with the Belgian Congo. We managed to cut handles from a luggage bag and knit them together to restart.

The car limped into Bunia and we spent the whole evening fashioning fan belts from luggage grip handles. These all gave way when driving back into Uganda. We finally bought shoe laces which, knotted together, enabled us to make it back home to Kampala.

Peter Lane, Nailsea, Somerset

Some forty years ago I took a young lady out in my MG for our first date. On our way home in a little lane near Lewes, East Sussex, the fan belt broke and I asked her if I could have her tights. She thought this was the oldest trick in the book, but agreed and I tied them on to the pulley wheels and limped home successfully.

We have now been happily married for 34 years and I have never had to ask again.

John Stone, Lidgate, Suffolk

I used to have an old VW Beetle in Germany where I was posted as an RAF navigator on F4s. After a meal with my pilot and his wife, I was about to drive home when the fan belt broke. "Don't worry," said the wife, raising her skirt and divesting herself of her tights, "these will get you home."

The plan worked for 5km, after which the tights melted and the engine caught fire. The car was a write-off — but it was worth it to see a nice pair of legs.

J. P. Smith, Ashwell, Rutland

Many years ago my family and I lived in Saudi Arabia. One weekend we were driven into the desert by some friends. In the middle of nowhere the car stopped: the fan belt had broken. We managed to get it to a small wayside stall festooned with fan belts of every size, but not the size we needed.

It was very cold and I was wearing tights under my trousers. I disappeared into the back of the truck and reappeared with the tights, which were duly cut to size and fitted to the bemusement of the stall staff. Nobody else believed it would work, but it did and we arrived home safely.

E. J. Woodall, Abingdon, Oxfordshire

How many Constable Constables and Sergeant Sergeants are there presently serving in police forces in the UK?

Richard Boother, Devizes, Wiltshire

While I cannot speak for the police services nationally, I can say that in the Met we have at least five people with the surname Constable and about twenty named Sergeant (of various spellings).

It must cause some confusion when a Constable Constable is promoted to sergeant, or when a Constable Sergeant is promoted and has to repeat themselves when required to state name and rank.

Amusing as such names may be, I do empathise. As a junior officer I was PC 123 O'Leary. Altogether now: sing along if you know the words!

Kevin O'Leary, Detective Chief Inspector, New Scotland Yard

I knew a Sergeant Major in the Army and had hoped that she would rise to the rank of Sergeant Major Major and maybe even get commissioned and become Major Major. General Major would have been even better because major-generals are two a penny.

Don Kent, Stanmore, Middlesex

My family are also Majors. Indeed on at least one guest night in mess there were present — all from the same regiment — a retired Brigadier Major, his son Major Major, and his grandson, a Lieutenant Major. My father and brother dealt with obvious jokes they received by saying: "You salute once for the rank, once for the name."

Patricia Thomas (née Major), Hindhead, Surrey

I have never known any police officers surnamed "Constable" or "Sergeant", but if I may digress, it was the practice in Leeds City Police to attempt humour in the allocation of collar numbers. So, for example, we had PC 4 Gott (reallocated 511 after a well-publicised memory lapse), though PC 1007 Bond was quickly renumbered 1000, supposedly because his mummy complained.

I was an anonymous 153. I have kin surnamed Commander but without aspiration to rank.

Mick Agar, Leeds

A few years ago, while being treated for a minor injury at St Thomas' Hospital in London, I noticed that the badge on the nurse attending me gave her surname as "Nurse". When I asked Nurse Nurse if her name had predisposed her to choosing such an apt occupation, she replied that she had never been able to be objective about it, so had never been sure. I did look for a "Doctor Doctor", but assumed that such a coincidence could not possibly be.

Amanda Woodham, Brighton

I can answer the question with some authority. I am Sergeant Peter Sergeant, currently serving in the Greater Manchester Police. My brother, Constable John Sergeant, serves in the Lancashire Constabulary. So it is not that rare after all.

It does create problems, and every time I answer the phone I await the inevitable quips.

Sergeant Peter Sergeant, Manchester

Why do people send in questions to newspapers, rather than looking on the internet? This is usually a quicker, easier and more satisfactory way of finding answers. (PS. There doesn't seem to be any answer to this particular question on the internet . . .)
David Hamill, Chiddingfold, Surrey

I would more readily accept the answer in *The Times* than one found on the internet. What was it my father always said? Believe nothing you hear and only half of what you see — and you won't go far wrong. An old chestnut coined with the internet in mind, surely.

Huw Beynon, Llandeilo, Dyfed

Might it be because they do not have access to a computer system?
Lance Jenkins, Hinxworth, Hertfordshire

The conclusion that I have come to is that it is because they wish to see their names in print. Of course, this also applies to those who send in answers . . .

(P.S. Once this reply has been published at thetimes.co.uk the answer to Mr Hamill's question will be available on the internet, should he wish to try again.)

John Webb, Pangbourne, Berkshire

INDEX OF WRITERS